HOW TO GROW OLD

ANCIENT WISDOM FOR MODERN READERS

■ ■ ■ ■

HOW TO
GROW OLD

■ ■ ■ ■ ■

Ancient Wisdom for the Second Half of Life

Marcus Tullius Cicero

Translated and with an introduction by
Philip Freeman

PRINCETON UNIVERSITY PRESS

PRINCETON AND OXFORD

Jacket art: Head of an Old Man (marble) (b/w photo), Roman
(1st century BC) / Palazzo Torlonia, Rome, Italy / Alinari /
Bridgeman Images

Library of Congress Cataloging-in-Publication Data

Names: Cicero, Marcus Tullius, author. | Freeman, Philip, 1961–
translator. | Cicero, Marcus Tullius. Cato maior de senectute. | Cicero,
Marcus Tullius. Cato maior de senectute. English.
Title: How to grow old : ancient wisdom for the second half of life /
Marcus Tullius Cicero ; translated and with an introduction by
Philip Freeman.
Description: Princeton : Princeton University Press, [2016] | In English
and Latin. | Includes bibliographical references.
Identifiers: LCCN 2015024460 | ISBN 9780691167701 (hardcover :
acid-free paper)
Subjects: LCSH: Old age—Early works to 1800.
Classification: LCC PA6308.C2 F7 2016 | DDC 305.26—dc23 LC record
available at http://lccn.loc.gov/2015024460

British Library Cataloging-in-Publication Data is available

This book has been composed in Garamond and Futura

Printed on acid-free paper. ∞

Printed in the United States of America

9 10 8

CONTENTS

INTRODUCTION

Forty-five BC was a bad year for Marcus Tullius Cicero.

The famous Roman orator and statesman was in his early sixties and alone. He had divorced his wife of thirty years not long before and married a younger woman, only to divorce her almost immediately. His beloved daughter Tullia had died at the beginning of the year, plunging Cicero into despair. And his place at the forefront of Roman politics had been lost just four years earlier when Julius Caesar crossed the Rubicon River and forced the Roman Republic into civil war. Cicero could not support Caesar and so, after initially standing against the new dictator and subsequently receiving a humiliating pardon, he had

retired to his country estate. There he remained, far from Rome, an old man in his own mind useless to the world.

But rather than sinking into his wine cups or committing suicide as his friend the younger Cato had done, Cicero turned to writing. He had been an avid student of Greek philosophy in his youth and longed to make his mark in the literary world by explaining to his Roman countrymen the ideas he had discovered in Plato, Aristotle, and other great thinkers. He was naturally inclined to the Stoic doctrines of virtue, order, and divine providence, as opposed to what he saw as the limited and self-indulgent views of the Epicureans. And so he began to write. In an astonishingly short period of time, working from early morning until late into the night, he produced numerous treatises on government, ethics,

education, religion, friendship, and moral duty.

Just before Caesar's murder on the Ides of March in 44 BC, Cicero turned to the subject of old age in a short treatise titled *De Senectute*. In the ancient world as in the modern, human life could be short, but we err when we suppose that the lifespan in Greece and Rome was necessarily brief. Although longevity in antiquity is notoriously difficult to measure, and infant and childhood mortality was certainly high, if men and women reached adulthood, they stood a decent chance of living into their sixties, seventies, or beyond.

Greek authors before Cicero had written about the last phase of life in different ways. Some idealized the elderly as enlightened bearers of wisdom, such as Homer's King Nestor, while others caricatured them as

tiresome and constant complainers. The poet Sappho from the sixth century BC is perhaps the most striking of all ancient writers on the subject as she mourns the loss of her own youth in a recently discovered fragmentary poem:

> . . . my skin once soft is wrinkled now,
> . . . my hair once black has turned to white.
> My heart has become heavy, my knees
> that once danced nimbly like fawns cannot
>   carry me.
> How often I lament these things—but what
>   can be done?
> No one who is human can escape old age.

Cicero, however, wanted to move beyond mere resignation to offer a broader picture of old age. While acknowledging its limitations, he sought to demonstrate that

the later years could be embraced as an opportunity for growth and completeness at the end of a life well lived. He chose as spokesman in his fictional dialogue the elder Cato, a Roman leader from the previous century whom he greatly admired. In his brief conversation with two younger friends, Cato shows how old age can be the best phase of life for those who apply themselves to living wisely. He refutes the objections of many critics that old age need be a wretched time of inactivity, illness, loss of sensual pleasure, and paralyzing fear about the closeness of death. Though Cicero pokes fun at seniors such as himself by having Cato digress into rambling asides (such as his extended discourse on farming), he nevertheless affirms old age as a time of life not to be dreaded but to be enjoyed to the fullest.

There are many valuable lessons to be learned from Cicero's little book on aging. Some of the most important are:

1. *A good old age begins in youth*. Cicero says the qualities that make the later years of our lives productive and happy should be cultivated from the beginning. Moderation, wisdom, clear thinking, enjoying all that life has to offer—these are habits we should learn while we are young since they will sustain us as we grow older. Miserable young people do not become happier as they grow older.

2. *Old age can be a wonderful part of life*. The senior years can be very enjoyable if we have developed the proper internal resources. Yes, there are plenty of unhappy old people, but they shouldn't blame age

for their problems. Their faults, Cicero says, are the result of poor character, not the number of years they have lived.

3. *There are proper seasons to life.* Nature has fashioned human life so that we enjoy certain things when we are young and others when we are older. Attempting to cling to youth after the appropriate time is useless. If you fight nature, you will lose.

4. *Older people have much to teach the young.* There is genuine wisdom in life that can be gained only by experience. It is our pleasure and duty as we grow older to pass this on to those younger than us who are willing to listen. But young people also can offer much to their elders, including the pleasure of their lively company.

5. *Old age need not deny us an active life, but we need to accept limitations.* No

eighty-year-old is going to win a foot race against healthy young people in their twenties, but we can still be physically active within the modest constraints imposed on us by our bodies. And there is so much older people can do that doesn't require great physical strength, from studying and writing to offering wisdom and experience to our communities.

6. *The mind is a muscle that must be exercised.* Cicero has the main character of his book learn Greek literature in his later years and carefully recall the events of the day before going to sleep each night. Whatever technique works, it is vital to use our minds as much as possible as we grow older.

7. *Older people must stand up for themselves.* Or as Cicero says, "Old age is respected only if it defends itself, maintains

its rights, submits to no one, and rules over its domain until its last breath." The later years of life are no time for passivity.

8. *Sex is highly overrated*. Not that older people can't enjoy the pleasures of the flesh, but the relentless sexual passions of youth fade as we grow older—and thank goodness they do, according to Cicero. The reduction of sensual appetites gives us room to enjoy other aspects of life that are much more satisfying and lasting.

9. *Cultivate your own garden*. Cicero presents this idea in his chapter praising the delights of farming, but there is an important lesson here. Finding a worthwhile activity in our later years that gives us true enjoyment is essential for happiness. Spreading manure or pruning grapevines may not be your passion, but whatever yours is, pursue it with joy.

10. *Death is not to be feared.* Cicero says that death marks either the end of human consciousness or the beginning of eternal bliss. Whether or not this is true, it certainly holds, as Cicero says, that life is like a play. A good actor knows when to leave the stage. To cling desperately to one's life when it has been lived well and is drawing to a close is both futile and foolish.

Readers from the Middle Ages to modern times have been delighted and inspired by Cicero's little book on aging. The French essayist Montaigne declared that it gave him an appetite for growing older, while the American Founding Father John Adams took pleasure in re-reading the dialogue many times in his later years. Benjamin Franklin was so impressed by the book that he printed a translation of it in Philadelphia

in 1744, making it one of the earliest classical works published in America. Today's
world, obsessed with the pursuit of youth,
needs Cicero's wisdom more than ever.

HOW TO GROW OLD

CATO MAIOR DE SENECTUTE

1. O Tite, si quid ego adiuero curamve
      levasso,
quae nunc te coquit et versat in pectore fixa,
ecquid erit praemi?

licet enim mihi versibus eisdem adfari te,
Attice, quibus adfatur Flamininum

   ille vir haud magna cum re, sed plenus
      fidei;

quamquam certo scio non, ut Flamininum

   sollicitari te, Tite, sic noctesque
      diesque,

HOW TO GROW OLD

Dedication to my friend Atticus

   1. Oh Titus, if I can give you any help,
   if I can lighten the cares fixed in your breast
   that now roast you and turn you on a spit,
   what will be my reward?[1]

And so, Atticus, may I address you in the
same lines which

   that man of little wealth but rich in loyalty

speaks to Flamininus—although I'm sure
that you're not like Flamininus

   who is tossed about by worry, Titus, day
      and night.

novi enim moderationem animi tui et aequitatem, teque non cognomen solum Athenis deportasse, sed humanitatem et prudentiam intellego. Et tamen te suspicor eisdem rebus quibus me ipsum interdum gravius commoveri, quarum consolatio et maior est et in aliud tempus differenda.

2. Nunc autem est mihi visum de senectute aliquid ad te conscribere. Hoc enim onere, quod mihi commune tecum est, aut iam urgentis aut certe adventantis senectutis et te et me etiam ipsum levari volo, etsi te quidem id modice ac sapienter, sicut omnia, et ferre et laturum esse certo scio; sed mihi, cum de senectute vellem aliquid scribere, tu occurrebas dignus eo munere quo uterque nostrum communiter uteretur. Mihi quidem

I know that you are a man of moderation and even temper, who brought home from Athens more than just a name![2] You brought back a cultured and prudent mind as well. Yet I suspect that you are troubled by the same political events of our day that are causing me such anxiety. But looking for comfort from such things is too difficult to do now and is a topic we'll have to put off until another time.

2. Instead, I would like to write something for you now about the subject of growing old. This burden is common to both of us—or at least it's quickly and unavoidably approaching—and I want to lighten the burden for you and me alike.[3] I know that you of course are facing the prospect of aging calmly and wisely, and that you will continue to do so in the future, just as you approach everything in life. But still,

ita iucunda huius libri confectio fuit ut non modo omnis absterserit senectutis molestias, sed effecerit mollem etiam et iucundam senectutem. Numquam igitur digne satis laudari philosophia poterit, cui qui pareat omne tempus aetatis sine molestia possit degere.

3. Sed de ceteris et diximus multa et saepe dicemus: hunc librum ad te de senectute misimus. Omnem autem sermonem tribuimus non Tithono, ut Aristo Ceus—parum enim esset auctoritatis in fabula—sed Marco Catoni seni, quo maiorem auctoritatem haberet oratio; apud quem Laelium et Scipionem facimus admirantis quod is tam facile

when I was thinking about writing on the subject, you kept coming to mind. I would like this little book to be a worthy gift that we can enjoy together. In fact, I've so much enjoyed composing this work that writing it has wiped away all thoughts of the disadvantages of growing older and made it instead seem a pleasant and enjoyable prospect.

We truly can't praise the love and pursuit of wisdom enough, since it allows a person to enjoy every stage of life free from worry.

3. I've written a great deal on other matters and will again in the future, but, as I said, this book that I'm sending you now is about growing old. When Aristo of Ceos wrote about the subject, he made Tithonus his spokesman, but I think it's wrong to give a mythological character such authority.[4] Instead, I have put my words into the

senectutem ferat, eisque eum responden-
tem. Qui si eruditius videbitur disputare
quam consuevit ipse in suis libris, attribuito
litteris Graecis, quarum constat eum per-
studiosum fuisse in senectute. Sed quid
opus est plura? Iam enim ipsius Catonis
sermo explicabit nostram omnem de senectute sententiam.

4. *Scipio*: Saepenumero admirari soleo
cum hoc Gaio Laelio cum ceterarum rerum
tuam excellentem, Marce Cato, perfectam-
que sapientiam, tum vel maxime quod numquam tibi senectutem gravem esse senserim,

mouth of the aged Marcus Cato so that they might be taken more seriously. I imagine Laelius and Scipio with him at his house, admiring how he is handling his age so well.[5] If he seems to reply in a way that is more learned than he appears in his own writings, attribute it to the Greek literature he studied carefully in his later years.

But why should I say more? From here on, the words of Cato himself will unfold to you my thoughts on growing older.

The Conversation with Cato

4. *Scipio*: When Gaius Laelius and I are talking, Marcus Cato, we often admire your outstanding and perfect wisdom in general, but more particularly that growing old never seems to be a burden to you. This is quite

quae plerisque senibus sic odiosa est, ut onus se Aetna gravius dicant sustinere.

Cato: Rem haud sane difficilem, Scipio et Laeli, admirari videmini; quibus enim nihil est in ipsis opis ad bene beateque vivendum, eis omnis aetas gravis est; qui autem omnia bona a se ipsi petunt, eis nihil malum potest videri quod naturae necessitas adferat. Quo in genere est in primis senectus; quam ut adipiscantur omnes optant, eandem accusant adeptam: tanta est stultitiae inconstantia atque perversitas. Obrepere aiunt eam citius quam putassent. Primum quis coegit eos falsum putare? Qui enim citius adulescentiae senectus quam pueritiae adulescentia obrepit? Deinde qui minus gravis esset eis senectus, si octingentesimum annum agerent, quam si octogesimum? Praeterita enim aetas quamvis longa,

different from the complaints of most older men, who claim that aging is a heavier load to bear than Mount Etna.[6]

Cato: I think, my young friends, that you are admiring me for something that isn't so difficult. Those who lack within themselves the means for living a blessed and happy life will find any age painful. But for those who seek good things within themselves, nothing imposed on them by nature will seem troublesome. Growing older is a prime example of this. Everyone hopes to reach old age, but when it comes, most of us complain about it. People can be so foolish and inconsistent.

They say that old age crept up on them much faster than they expected. But, first of all, who is to blame for such poor judgment? Does old age steal upon youth any faster

cum effluxisset, nulla consolatione permulcere posset stultam senectutem.

5. Quocirca si sapientiam meam admirari soletis (quae utinam digna esset opinione vestra nostroque cognomine!), in hoc sumus sapientes, quod naturam optimam ducem tamquam deum sequimur eique paremus; a qua non veri simile est, cum ceterae partes aetatis bene descriptae sint, extremum actum tamquam ab inerti poeta esse neglectum. Sed tamen necesse fuit esse aliquid extremum, et tamquam in arborum bacis terraeque fructibus, maturitate tempestiva quasi vietum et caducum, quod ferundum est molliter sapienti. Quid est enim aliud Gigantum modo bellare cum dis, nisi naturae repugnare?

than youth does on childhood? Would growing old really be less of a burden to them if they were approaching eight hundred rather than eighty? If old people are foolish, nothing can console them for time slipping away, no matter how long they live.

5. So if you compliment me on being wise—and I wish I were worthy of that estimate and my name[7]—in this way alone do I deserve it: I follow nature as the best guide and obey her like a god. Since she has carefully planned the other parts of the drama of life, it's unlikely that she would be a bad playwright and neglect the final act. And this last act must take place, as surely as the fruits of trees and the earth must someday wither and fall. But a wise person knows this and accepts it with grace. Fighting against nature is as pointless as the battles of the giants against the gods.[8]

6. *Laelius*: Atqui, Cato, gratissimum nobis (ut etiam pro Scipione pollicear) feceris, si, quoniam speramus—volumus quidem certe senes fieri, multo ante a te didicerimus quibus facillime rationibus ingravescentem aetatem ferre possimus.

Cato: Faciam vero, Laeli, praesertim si utrique vestrum, ut dicis, gratum futurum est.

Laelius: Volumus sane nisi molestum est, Cato, tamquam longam aliquam viam confeceris, quam nobis quoque ingrediundum sit, istuc quo pervenisti videre quale sit.

7. *Cato*: Faciam ut potero, Laeli. Saepe enim interfui querelis aequalium meorum— pares autem, vetere proverbio cum paribus facillime congregantur. Quae Gaius Salinator, quae Spurius Albinus, homines consulares nostri fere aequales, deplorare solebant—

6. *Laelius*: True, Cato, but we have a special request to make of you—and I think I speak for Scipio as well. We both hope to live long enough to become old someday, so we would be very grateful if you could teach us even now how we can most reasonably bear the weight of the approaching years.

Cato: It would be my pleasure, Laelius, if you would really like me to.

Laelius: We would indeed, if it's not too much trouble. You've already traveled far on the road we will follow, so we would like to learn about the journey from you.

7. *Cato*: I'll do my best. I have often heard the complaints of people my age—"like gathers with like," says the old proverb—especially Gaius Salinator and Spurius Albinus, my near-contemporaries and former consuls, who were constantly moaning about

tum quod voluptatibus carerent sine quibus vitam nullam putarent, tum quod spernerentur ab eis a quibus essent coli soliti. Qui mihi non id videbantur accusare quod esset accusandum; nam si id culpa senectutis accideret, eadem mihi usu venirent, reliquisque omnibus maioribus natu; quorum ego multorum cognovi senectutem sine querela, qui se et libidinum vinculis laxatos esse non moleste ferrent, nec a suis despicerentur. Sed omnium istius modi querelarum in moribus est culpa, non in aetate. Moderati enim et nec difficiles nec inhumani senes tolerabilem senectutem agunt, importunitas autem et inhumanitas omni aetati molesta est.

how age had snatched away the sensual pleasures of life, pleasures without which—at least to them—life was not worth living.[9] Then they complained that they were being neglected by those who had once paid them attention. But in my view, their blame was misplaced. If aging were the real problem, then the same ills would have befallen me and every other old person. But I have known many people who have grown old without complaint, who don't miss the binding chains of sensual passion, and who aren't neglected by their friends. Again, the blame for all these sorts of complaints is a matter of character, not of age. Older people who are reasonable, good-tempered, and gracious will bear aging well. Those who are mean-spirited and irritable will be unhappy at every period of their lives.

8. *Laelius*: Est, ut dicis, Cato; sed fortasse dixerit quispiam tibi propter opes et copias et dignitatem tuam tolerabiliorem senectutem videri, id autem non posse multis contingere.

Cato: Est istuc quidem, Laeli, aliquid, sed nequaquam in isto sunt omnia; ut Themistocles fertur Seriphio cuidam in iurgio respondisse, cum ille dixisset non eum sua, sed patriae gloria splendorem adsecutum: 'Nec hercule,' inquit, 'si ego Seriphius essem, nec tu, si Atheniensis clarus umquam fuisses.' Quod eodem modo de senectute dici potest: nec enim in summa inopia levis esse senectus potest ne sapienti quidem, nec insipienti etiam in summa copia non gravis.

8. *Laelius*: That is undoubtedly true, Cato. But what if someone were to say that your wealth, property, and social standing—advantages in life that few people possess—are what have made growing older so pleasant for you?

Cato: There is some truth in that, Laelius, but it isn't the whole story. Remember the tale of Themistocles and the man from Seriphos.[10] The two were having an argument one day during which the Seriphian said that Themistocles was famous only because of the glory of his city, not his own achievements. "By Hercules, that's true," said Themistocles. "I would never have been famous if I was from Seriphos—nor you if you were from Athens." The same can be said of old age. It isn't a light burden if a person, even a wise man, is poor. But if someone is

9. Aptissima omnino sunt, Scipio et Laeli, arma senectutis artes exercitationesque virtutum; quae in omni aetate cultae, cum diu multumque vixeris, mirificos ecferunt fructus; non solum quia numquam deserunt ne extremo quidem tempore aetatis (quamquam id quidem maximum est), verum etiam quia conscientia bene actae vitae multorumque bene factorum recordatio iucundissima est.

10. Ego Quintus Maximum, eum qui Tarentum recepit, senem adulescens ita dilexi, ut aequalem; erat enim in illo viro comitate condita gravitas, nec senectus mores mutaverat. Quamquam eum colere coepi non admodum grandem natu, sed tamen iam aetate provectum. Anno enim

a fool, all the money in the world won't make aging easier.

9. My dear Scipio and Laelius, old age has its own appropriate defenses, namely, the study and practice of wise and decent living. If you cultivate these in every period of your life, then when you grow old they will yield a rich harvest. Not only will they produce wondrous fruit even at the very end of life—a key point in our discussion—but you will be satisfied to know that you have lived your life well and have many happy memories of these good deeds.

10. When I was young, I was fond of Quintus Maximus, who recaptured Tarentum, as if we were the same age, although he was an old man and I just a lad.[11] He was a man of dignity seasoned with friendliness, and age had not changed him. When I first began to get to know him, he was not yet of

post consul primum fuerat quam ego natus
sum, cumque eo quartum consule adules-
centulus miles ad Capuam profectus sum
quintoque anno post ad Tarentum. Quaestor
deinde quadriennio post factus sum, quem
magistratum gessi consulibus Tuditano et
Cethego, cum quidem ille admodum senex
suasor legis Cinciae de donis et muneribus
fuit. Hic et bella gerebat ut adulescens, cum
plane grandis esset, et Hannibalem iuveni-
liter exsultantem patientia sua molliebat; de
quo praeclare familiaris noster Ennius:

unus homo nobis cunctando restituit rem,
non enim rumores ponebat ante salutem:
ergo plusque magisque viri nunc gloria
    claret.

great old age but certainly growing advanced in years. He had first become a consul the year after I was born. In his fourth term as consul, I was a young soldier marching with him to Capua, then five years later to Tarentum. Four years after that, when Tuditanus and Cethegus were consuls, I became a quaestor. At that same time Quintus Maximus was giving speeches in favor of the Cincian Law on gifts and rewards, though he was quite elderly by then.[12]

Even though he was old, he waged war like a young man, and wore down Hannibal's youthful exuberance by his persistence. My friend Ennius spoke splendidly about him:

One man, by delaying, saved our country.
He refused to put his reputation above the
    safety of Rome,
so that now his glory grows ever brighter.

11. Tarentum vero qua vigilantia, quo consilio recepit! cum quidem me audiente Salinatori, qui amisso oppido fugerat in arcem, glorianti atque ita dicenti; 'Mea opera, Quinte Fabi, Tarentum recepisti,' 'Certe,' inquit ridens, 'nam nisi tu amisisses numquam recepissem.' Nec vero in armis praestantior quam in toga; qui consul iterum Spurio Carvilio conlega quiescente Gaio Flaminio tribuno plebis, quoad potuit restitit agrum Picentem et Gallicum viritim contra senatus auctoritatem dividenti; augurque cum esset, dicere ausus est optimis auspiciis ea geri, quae pro rei publicae salute gererentur, quae contra rem publicam ferrentur, contra auspicia ferri.

11. Such vigilance and skill he displayed in recapturing Tarentum! I myself heard Salinator—the Roman commander who had lost the town and fled to the citadel—boast to him, "Quintus Fabius, you owe the retaking of Tarentum to me."[13] The general laughed and said in reply, "That's certainly true, since I wouldn't have had to recapture it if you hadn't lost it in the first place."

Nor was Fabius more distinguished as a soldier than as a statesman. When he was consul the second time, the tribune Gaius Flaminius was trying to parcel out Picene and Gallic land against the express will of the Senate. Even though his colleague Spurius Carvilius kept silent, Fabius made every effort to oppose Flaminius.[14] And when he was an augur, he dared to say that the auspices favored whatever was for the good of

12. Multa in eo viro praeclara cognovi, sed nihil admirabilius, quam quo modo ille mortem fili tulit clari viri et consularis; est in manibus laudatio, quam cum legimus, quem philosophum non contemnimus? Nec vero ille in luce modo atque in oculis civium magnus, sed intus domique praestantior: qui sermo, quae praecepta, quanta notitia antiquitatis, scientia iuris auguri! Multae etiam, ut in homine Romano litterae; omnia memoria tenebat, non domestica solum sed etiam externa bella. Cuius sermone ita tum cupide fruebar, quasi iam divinarem, id quod evenit, illo exstincto, fore unde discerem neminem.

the state and that what was bad for the state was against the auspices.[15]

12. I can assure you from personal observation that there were many admirable qualities in that man, but nothing was more striking than how he bore the death of his son, a distinguished former consul. His funeral oration is available for us to read, and when we do, what philosopher is not put to shame? But Fabius wasn't just commendable in public while under the gaze of his fellow citizens. He was even more admirable in the privacy of his own home. His conversation, his moral advice, his knowledge of history, his expertise in the laws of augury—all were astonishing! He was very well read for a Roman, and knew everything not only about our own wars but also about foreign conflicts. I was eager to listen to him at the time, as if I foresaw, as indeed

13. Quorsum igitur haec tam multa de Maximo? Quia profecto videtis, nefas esse dictu miseram fuisse talem senectutem. Nec tamen omnes possunt esse Scipiones aut Maximi, ut urbium expugnationes, ut pedestres navalesve pugnas, ut bella a se gesta, ut triumphos recordentur; est etiam quiete et pure atque eleganter actae aetatis placida ac lenis senectus, qualem accepimus Platonis, qui uno et octogesimo anno scribens est mortuus; qualem Isocratis, qui eum librum qui Panathenaicus inscribitur quarto et nonagesimo anno scripsisse se dicit, vixitque quinquennium postea; cuius magister Leontinus Gorgias centum et septem complevit annos neque umquam in suo studio atque opere cessavit. Qui, cum ex eo quaereretur, cur tam diu vellet esse in vita, 'Nihil

happened, that when he was gone I would have no one else to learn from.

13. Why have I said so much about Fabius Maximus? So that you might see how wrong it would be to describe an old age like his as unhappy. Of course, not everyone is able to be a Scipio or a Fabius and talk about the cities they have conquered, the battles they have fought on land or sea, the wars they have waged, and the triumphs they have won. But there is another kind of old age, the peaceful and serene end of a life spent quietly, blamelessly, and with grace. Plato lived this way in his last years, still writing when he died at eighty-one.[16] Isocrates is another example, who tells us himself he was ninety-four when he composed his *Panathenaicus*—and he lived another five years after that![17] His teacher Gorgias of Leontini reached his one hundred and

habeo,' inquit, 'quod accusem senectutem.'
Praeclarum responsum et docto homine
dignum.

14. Sua enim vitia insipientes et suam
culpam in senectutem conferunt. Quod
non faciebat is cuius modo mentionem feci
Ennius:

> sicuti fortis equus, spatio qui saepe supremo
> vicit Olympia, nunc senio confectus
>   quiescit.

Equi fortis et victoris senectuti comparat
suam. Quem quidem probe meminisse
potestis; anno enim undevicesimo post eius
mortem hi consules, T. Flamininus et M'.
Acilius, facti sunt; ille autem Caepione et
Philippo iterum consulibus mortuus est,

seventh birthday, never resting from his studies and work.[18] When someone asked him why he wished to live so long, he replied, "I have no reason to complain about old age." A noble answer, worthy of a scholar.

14. Foolish people blame old age for their own faults and shortcomings. Ennius, whom I mentioned just a little while ago, certainly didn't do this, for he compares himself as an old man to a gallant and victorious racehorse:

> Like a courageous steed that has often won
> Olympic races
> in the last lap, now weakened by age he
> takes his rest.

You probably remember Ennius quite clearly, for he died only nineteen years before the election of our present consuls,

cum ego quinque et sexaginta annos natus legem Voconiam magna voce et bonis lateribus suasi. Sed annos septuaginta natus, tot enim vixit Ennius, ita ferebat duo quae maxima putantur onera, paupertatem et senectutem, ut eis paene delectari videretur.

15. Etenim cum complector animo, quattuor reperio causas cur senectus misera videatur:

unam, quod avocet a rebus gerendis.
alteram, quod corpus faciat infirmius.
tertiam, quod privet fere omnibus voluptatibus.
quartam, quod haud procul absit a morte.

Titus Flamininus and Manius Acilius, back when Caepio and Philippus were consuls (the latter for the second time). I was sixty-five when he died and I made a speech in favor of the Voconian Law with a loud voice and mighty lungs.[19] Ennius was seventy at the time and suffered what men suppose are the two greatest burdens of life—poverty and old age. But he bore them so well you might think he enjoyed them.

15. When I think about old age, I can find four reasons why people consider it so miserable:

First, because it takes us away from an active life.
Second, because it weakens the body.
Third, because it deprives us of almost all sensual pleasures.
Fourth, because it is not far from death.

Earum, si placet, causarum quanta quamque sit iusta unaquaeque videamus.

A rebus gerendis senectus abstrahit. Quibus? An eis, quae iuventute geruntur et viribus? Nullaene igitur res sunt seniles, quae vel infirmis corporibus, animo tamen administrentur? Nihil ergo agebat Quintus Maximus, nihil Lucius Paulus pater tuus, socer optimi viri fili mei? Ceteri senes, Fabricii Curii Coruncanii, cum rem publicam consilio et auctoritate defendebant, nihil agebant?

If you don't mind, let's look at each of these reasons one by one to see if they are true.

The Active Life

Let's consider first the claim that old age denies us an active life. What kind of activities are we talking about? Don't we mean the sort we engage in when young and strong? But surely there are activities suitable for older minds even when the body is weakened. Wasn't there important work for Quintus Maximus, whom I mentioned earlier, and for Lucius Paullus, your own father, Scipio, and also the father-in-law of that best of men, my son?[20] And what about other old men, such as Fabricius, Curius, and Coruncanius?[21] Were they doing nothing when they were using their wisdom and influence to protect their country?

16. Ad Appi Claudi senectutem accedebat etiam ut caecus esset; tamen is cum sententia senatus inclinaret ad pacem cum Pyrrho foedusque faciendum, non dubitavit dicere illa, quae versibus persecutus est Ennius:

quo vobis mentes, rectae quae stare solebant
antehac, dementis sese flexere viai?

ceteraque gravissime; notum enim vobis carmen est, et tamen ipsius Appi exstat oratio. Atque haec ille egit septimo decimo anno post alterum consulatum, cum inter duos consulatus anni decem interfuissent, censorque ante superiorem consulatum fuisset; ex quo intellegitur, Pyrrhi bello grandem sane fuisse; et tamen sic a patribus accepimus.

16. Appius Claudius was not only old but also blind when he spoke before the Senate, which was favoring a peace treaty with King Pyrrhus.[22] Yet he did not hesitate to utter the words Ennius later put into verse:

What madness has turned your minds, once firm
and strong, from their course?

And so on, in the most impressive style. But you know the poem, and indeed the actual speech of Appius survives. He delivered it seventeen years after his second consulship—though there were ten years between his consulships and he had been censor before first being consul—so you can see that he was a very old man by the time of the war with Pyrrhus. Yet this is the story recorded by our ancestors.

17. Nihil igitur adferunt qui in re gerenda versari senectutem negant, similesque sunt ut si qui gubernatorem in navigando nihil agere dicant, cum alii malos scandant, alii per foros cursent, alii sentinam exhauriant, ille autem clavum tenens quietus sedeat in puppi. Non faciat ea quae iuvenes; at vero multo maiora et meliora facit. Non viribus aut velocitate aut celeritate corporum res magnae geruntur, sed consilio auctoritate sententia; quibus non modo non orbari, sed etiam augeri senectus solet.

18. Nisi forte ego vobis, qui et miles et tribunus et legatus et consul versatus sum in vario genere bellorum, cessare nunc videor cum bella non gero: at senatui quae sint gerenda praescribo et quomodo; Carthagini

17. People who say there are no useful activities for old age don't know what they're talking about. They are like those who say a pilot does nothing useful for sailing a ship because others climb the masts, run along the gangways, and work the pumps while he sits quietly in the stern holding the rudder. He may not be doing what the younger crewmen are doing, but what he does is much more important and valuable. It's not by strength or speed or swiftness of body that great deeds are done, but by wisdom, character, and sober judgment. These qualities are not lacking in old age but in fact grow richer as time passes.

18. In my life I have served as a soldier in the ranks, then a junior officer, then a general, and finally, when consul, as a commander-in-chief. Since I am no longer fighting in wars, perhaps you think I am

male iam diu cogitanti bellum multo ante denuntio, de qua vereri non ante desinam, quam illam exscissam esse cognovero.

19. Quam palmam utinam di immortales, Scipio, tibi reservent, ut avi reliquias persequare! cuius a morte tertius hic et tricesimus annus est, sed memoriam illius viri omnes excipient anni consequentes; anno ante me censorem mortuus est, novem annis post meum consulatum cum consul iterum me consule creatus esset. Num igitur si ad centesimum annum vixisset, senectutis eum suae paeniteret? Nec enim excursione nec saltu nec eminus hastis aut comminus gladiis uteretur, sed consilio ratione sententia; quae nisi essent in senibus, non summum consilium maiores nostri appellassent senatum.

doing nothing. But the Senate listens to me when I speak about which wars to fight and how to fight them. Even now, I am looking into the future and planning war on Carthage. I will never stop fearing that city until I know it has been totally destroyed.[23]

19. And I pray that the immortal gods will reserve for you, Scipio, the honor of completing the work your grandfather left unfinished. It has been thirty-three years since that greatest of men died, but each passing year will increase the memory of his fame. He died the year before I became censor, nine years after my consulship, during which time he himself was elected consul a second time.

If your grandfather had lived to be a hundred, would he have regretted his old age? Certainly not. He wouldn't have spent such time running or jumping or throwing

20. Apud Lacedaemonios quidem ei qui amplissimum magistratum gerunt, ut sunt sic etiam nominantur senes. Quodsi legere aut audire voletis externa, maximas res publicas ab adulescentibus labefactatas, a senibus sustentatas et restitutas reperietis:

Cedo qui vestram rem publicam tantam amisistis tam cito?

sic enim percontantur in Naevi poetae Ludo. Respondentur et alia et hoc in primis:

his spear or practicing with his sword, but instead he would have used his wisdom, reason, and judgment. If old men didn't possess these qualities, our ancestors never would have given the name "Senate" to our highest council.[24]

20. Among the Spartans as well, those who hold the most important offices are called "elders," which is exactly what they are. If you read or listen to the histories of foreign lands, you will learn that the greatest states were overturned by the young but saved and restored by the old. As Naevius says in his play *The Game*:[25]

Tell me, how did you lose your great nation
    so quickly?

And the most significant answer the characters give is this:

proveniebant oratores novi, stulti
   adulescentuli.

Temeritas est videlicet florentis aetatis, prudentia senescentis.

21. At memoria minuitur.—Credo, nisi
eam exerceas, aut etiam si sis natura tardior.
Themistocles omnium civium perceperat
nomina; num igitur censetis eum, cum aetate processisset, qui Aristides esset, Lysi-
machum salutare solitum? Equidem non
modo eos novi qui sunt, sed eorum patres
etiam et avos; nec sepulcra legens vereor,
quod aiunt, ne memoriam perdam; eis enim
ipsis legendis in memoriam redeo mortuo-
rum. Nec vero quemquam senem audivi
oblitum quo loco thesaurum obruisset; omnia
quae curant meminerunt, vadimonia constituta, quis sibi, cui ipsi debeant.

> Because new speakers came forth, foolish
> young men.

Rashness is truly the fruit of youth, but wisdom of old age.

21. Some people will say that memory fades away as the years pass. Of course it does if you don't exercise it or aren't very bright to begin with. Themistocles learned by heart the names of all the citizens of Athens. So when he grew old, do you think he confused Aristides with Lysimachus when he greeted them?[26] I myself remember not only those who are living now but their fathers and grandfathers too. As I read their epitaphs, I am not afraid of losing my memory, as the superstition says, but rather find my recollections of the dead refreshed. And I have certainly never heard of an old man who forgot where he hid his money!

22. Quid iurisconsulti, quid pontifices, quid augures, quid philosophi senes, quam multa meminerunt! Manent ingenia senibus, modo permaneat studium et industria, neque ea solum in claris et honoratis viris, sed in vita etiam privata et quieta. Sophocles ad summam senectutem tragoedias fecit; quod propter studium cum rem neglegere familiarem videretur, a filiis in iudicium vocatus est, ut quemadmodum nostro more male rem gerentibus patribus bonis interdici solet, sic illum quasi desipientem a re familiari removerent iudices; tum senex dicitur eam fabulam quam in manibus habebat et proxime scripserat, Oedipum Coloneum, recitasse iudicibus quaesisseque, num illud

Old people remember what interests them, whether it be the dates to appear in court, who owes them money, or to whom they owe money.

22. And what about elderly lawyers, priests, augurs, and philosophers? What a multitude of things they remember! Old people maintain a sound mind as long as they remain eager to learn and apply themselves. This is true not only of public figures but of those leading quiet, private lives. Sophocles composed tragedies long into his old age.[27] When he seemed to be neglecting his family's finances because of his passion for writing, his sons took him to court so that the jurymen could remove him from authority on account of his weakness of mind (like us, they had laws empowering such actions when the head of the family was mismanaging business affairs). They say

carmen desipientis videretur; quo recitato sententiis iudicum est liberatus.

23. Num igitur hunc, num Homerum, Hesiodum Simonidem Stesichorum, num quos ante dixi Isocratem Gorgian, num philosophorum principes Pythagoram Democritum, num Platonem, num Xenocratem, num postea Zenonem Cleanthem aut eum quem vos etiam vidistis Romae, Diogenem Stoicum coegit in suis studiis obmutescere senectus? an in omnibus his studiorum agitatio vitae aequalis fuit?

24. Age ut ista divina studia omittamus, possum nominare ex agro Sabino rusticos Romanos, vicinos et familiares meos, quibus

that the old man then read to the court his *Oedipus at Colonus,* which he had just written and was even then revising, asking when he finished if it sounded like the work of a weak-minded person. After his recitation, the jury acquitted him.

23. Clearly Sophocles was not deterred in his calling by old age, nor were Homer, Hesiod, Simonides, or Stesichorus, nor the two men I mentioned earlier, Isocrates and Gorgias, not to mention outstanding philosophers such as Pythagoras, Democritus, Plato, Xenocrates, or their successors Zeno, Cleanthes, or Diogenes the Stoic, whom you have both seen at Rome.[28] Didn't they all actively pursue their work as long as they lived?

24. But setting aside these extraordinary men and their work, I can name for you elderly Roman farmers from the Sabine

absentibus numquam fere ulla in agro maiora opera fiunt, non serendis, non percipiendis, non condendis fructibus; quamquam in aliis minus hoc mirum est—nemo est enim tam senex qui se annum non putet posse vivere—sed idem in eis elaborant quae sciunt nihil ad se omnino pertinere:

serit arbores quae alteri saeculo prosient,

ut ait Statius noster in Synephebis.

25. Nec vero dubitat agricola, quamvis sit senex, quaerenti cui serat respondere, 'dis immortalibus, qui me non accipere modo haec a maioribus voluerunt, sed etiam posteris prodere.'

Et melius Caecilius de sene 'alteri saeculo' prospiciente, quam illud idem:

countryside, my own neighbors and friends, who are almost never out of their fields during major farming operations such as sowing, reaping, and storing crops. Although their work is less notable than some other types of labor—for truly no one is so old that he doesn't think he'll live another year— these men know they are working at tasks they will not live to see finished. As Caecilius Statius says in his *Young Comrades:*[29]

He plants trees for the use of another age.

25. If you ask a farmer, however old he might be, whom he is planting for, he will always reply: "For the immortal gods, who have not only handed down to me these things from my ancestors but also determined that I should pass them on to my descendants."

edepol Senectus, si nil quicquam aliud viti
apportes tecum, cum advenis unum id sat
    est,
quod diu vivendo multa quae non vult
    videt.

et multa fortasse quae vult; atque in ea quae
non vult saepe etiam adulescentia incurrit.
Illud vero idem Caecilius vitiosius:

tum equidem in senecta hoc deputo
    miserrimum,
sentire ea aetate eumpse esse odiosum alteri.

When he wrote about that old man making provisions for future generations, Caecilius said something even more striking:

> Indeed, Old Age, if you brought no evil
> but this alone, it would be enough—that a person
> by living long sees many things he does not wish to see.

But perhaps the same old man sees much he likes! In any case, even young people see much in life they wish they hadn't.

Another sentiment expressed by Caecilius is even worse:

> I think the most unhappy thing about old age
> is feeling that you are wearisome to the young.

26. Iucundum potius quam odiosum: ut enim adulescentibus bona indole praeditis sapientes senes delectantur, leviorque fit senectus eorum qui a iuventute coluntur et diliguntur, sic adulescentes senum praeceptis gaudent, quibus ad virtutum studia ducuntur; nec minus intellego me vobis quam mihi vos esse iucundos.

Sed videtis ut senectus non modo languida atque iners non sit, verum etiam sit operosa et semper agens aliquid et moliens, tale scilicet quale cuiusque studium in superiore vita fuit. Quid qui etiam addiscunt aliquid, ut et Solonem versibus gloriantem videmus, qui se cotidie aliquid addiscentem dicit senem fieri, et ego feci qui litteras Graecas senex didici? Quas quidem sic avide arripui, quasi diuturnam sitim explere cupiens, ut ea ipsa mihi nota essent quibus me nunc exemplis uti videtis. Quod cum

26. Not at all, I say! The old can be a pleasure rather than a burden. Just as wise old men enjoy the company of young men of good character and find their old age made lighter by honor and affection received from the young, so young men rejoice in the instruction given by old men, by which they are led to virtue. My young friends, I like to think you enjoy my company as much as I do yours.

So you see how old age, far from being feeble and sluggish, can be very active, always doing and engaged in something, as it follows the pursuits of earlier years. And you should never stop learning, just as Solon in his poetry boasts that while growing old he learned something new every day.[30] I've done the same, teaching myself Greek as an old man. I have seized on this study like someone trying to satisfy a long

fecisse Socratem in fidibus audirem, vellem equidem etiam illud (discebant enim fidibus antiqui) sed in litteris certe elaboravi.

27. Ne nunc quidem vires desidero adulescentis (is enim erat locus alter de vitiis senectutis), non plus quam adulescens tauri aut elephanti desiderabam. Quod est, eo decet uti, et quidquid agas agere pro viribus. Quae enim vox potest esse contemptior quam Milonis Crotoniatae? Qui cum iam senex esset, athletasque se exercentes in curriculo videret, aspexisse lacertos suos dicitur, illacrimansque dixisse 'at hi quidem mortui iam sunt.' Non vero tam isti quam

thirst. (And this, by the way, is how I've been able to use all the examples I've brought into this discussion.) I have heard that Socrates learned as an old man to play the lyre, that favorite instrument of the ancients. I wish I could do that as well, but at least I've applied myself diligently to literature.

The Body and the Mind

27. I no longer wish for the strength of youth—that was the second objection to growing older we listed—any more than when I was a young man I desired the strength of a bull or an elephant. People should use the strength they have appropriately whatever their age. What story could be more pitiful than that of Milo of Croton?[31] One day when as an old man he was watching the young athletes training on the racecourse, he reportedly looked

tu ipse, nugator; neque enim ex te umquam es nobilitatus, sed ex lateribus et lacertis tuis. Nihil Sextus Aelius tale, nihil multis annis ante Tiberius Coruncanius, nihil modo Publio Crassus, a quibus iura civibus praescribebantur; quorum usque ad extremum spiritum est provecta prudentia.

28. Orator metuo ne languescat senectute; est enim munus eius non ingeni solum, sed laterum etiam et virium. Omnino canorum illud in voce splendescit etiam nescioquo pacto in senectute; quod equidem adhuc non amisi, et videtis annos. Sed tamen est decorus seni sermo quietus et remissus, facitque persaepe ipsa sibi audientiam diserti senis compta et mitis oratio. Quam si ipse

down at his own muscles and wept, saying: "And these now are dead." But not as dead as you, foolish man! For your fame never came from yourself, only from the strength of your sides and arms.

Sextus Aelius, Tiberius Coruncanius of earlier times, and, more recently, Publius Crassus were very different from this. These men instructed their fellow citizens in the law and remained expert jurists until their last breath.[32]

28. I do fear that a public speaker loses some of his effectiveness as he grows older, since his skill depends not only on his intellect but also on his lungs and strength. But advancing years do have a way of making the voice brighter, more melodious. I haven't yet lost this quality and you can see how old I am. The appropriate speaking style of later years is peaceful and restrained, and

exsequi nequeas, possis tamen Scipioni prae-
cipere et Laelio; quid enim est iucundius
senectute stipata studiis iuventutis?

29. An ne tales quidem vires senectuti re-
linquemus, ut adulescentis doceat, instit-
uat, ad omne offici munus instruat? Quo
quidem opere quid potest esse praeclarius?
Mihi vero et Gnaeus et Publius Scipiones
et avi tui duo, Lucius Aemilius et Publius
Africanus, comitatu nobilium iuvenum for-
tunati videbantur; nec ulli bonarum artium
magistri non beati putandi, quamvis con-
senuerint vires atque defecerint; etsi ipsa
ista defectio virium adulescentiae vitiis efficitur saepius quam senectutis: libidinosa
enim et intemperans adulescentia effetum
corpus tradit senectuti.

often the calm and elegant voice of an older person lends itself to being more readily heard. And even if someone is no longer able to speak well, he can still instruct a Scipio or a Laelius!

29. What indeed could be more pleasant than an old age surrounded by the enthusiasm of youth? For surely we must agree that old people at least have the strength to teach the young and prepare them for the many duties of life. What responsibility could be more honorable than this? Truly, it seemed to me, Scipio, that Gnaeus and Publius Scipio, as well as your two grandfathers, Lucius Aemilius and Publius Africanus, were most fortunate to be accompanied always by crowds of noble young people.[33]

And no one who provides a liberal education to others can be considered unhappy

30. Cyrus quidem apud Xenophontem, eo sermone quem moriens habuit, cum admodum senex esset, negat se umquam sensisse senectutem suam imbecilliorem factam quam adulescentia fuisset. Ego Lucium Metellum memini puer, qui cum quadriennio post alterum consulatum pontifex maximus factus esset, viginti et duos annos ei sacerdotio praefuit, ita bonis esse viribus extremo tempore aetatis, ut adulescentiam non requireret. Nihil necesse est mihi de me ipso dicere—quamquam est id quidem senile aetatique nostrae conceditur.

31. Videtisne ut apud Homerum saepissime Nestor de virtutibus suis praedicet?

even if his body is failing with age. The excesses of youth are more often to blame for the loss of bodily strength than old age. A wanton and wasteful youth yields to old age a worn-out body.

30. The elderly Cyrus, according to Xenophon, declared as an old man on his deathbed that he had never felt less vigorous in his later years than as a young man.[34] And also I remember as a boy seeing Lucius Metellus, who, four years after his second consulship, became chief priest and held that post for twenty-two years.[35] To the end of his days he was so vigorous that in spite of extreme old age he never felt the loss of youth. I don't need to mention myself in this respect, though old men like me are allowed to indulge themselves.

31. Don't you see in Homer how often Nestor declares his own admirable qualities?[36]

Iam enim tertiam aetatem hominum vide-
bat; nec erat ei verendum ne vera praedi-
cans de se nimis videretur aut insolens aut
loquax. Etenim, ut ait Homerus, 'ex eius
lingua melle dulcior fluebat oratio'; quam
ad suavitatem nullis egebat corporis viribus. Et tamen dux ille Graeciae nusquam
optat ut Aiacis similes habeat decem, sed ut
Nestoris; quod si sibi acciderit, non dubitat
quin brevi sit Troia peritura.

32. Sed redeo ad me: quartum ago annum
et octogesimum. Vellem equidem idem possem gloriari quod Cyrus; sed tamen hoc
queo dicere, non me quidem eis esse viribus
quibus aut miles bello Punico aut quaestor
eodem bello aut consul in Hispania fuerim,
aut quadriennio post cum tribunus milita-
ris depugnavi apud Thermopylas Manio
Acilio Glabrione consule; sed tamen ut vos

He had seen three generations of men at that point in his life, but he didn't fear seeming overly talkative or conceited when he spoke the truth about himself. For as Homer says: "Speech sweeter than honey flowed from his tongue."[37] Now this sweetness in no way depended on his physical strength — and yet the Greek leader Agamemnon never prays for ten men like Ajax, but for ten like Nestor.[38] He doesn't doubt that if he had them, Troy would quickly fall.

32. But to return to myself. I am eighty-four years old now, and I wish I could make the same boast as Cyrus. But this much I can say: I no longer have the energy I did when I served as a young soldier in the Punic War, or as quaestor in the same war, or as a consul and general in Spain, or four years later, serving as a military tribune in the campaign at Thermopylae under the

videtis, non plane me enervavit, non adflixit senectus; non curia vires meas desiderat, non rostra, non amici, non clientes, non hospites. Nec enim umquam sum adsensus veteri illi laudatoque proverbio, quod monet mature fieri senem si diu velis senex esse; ego vero me minus diu senem esse mallem, quam esse senem antequam essem. Itaque nemo adhuc convenire me voluit cui fuerim occupatus.

33. At minus habeo virium quam vestrum utervis. Ne vos quidem Titi Ponti centurionis vires habetis; num idcirco est ille praestantior? Moderatio modo virium adsit, et tantum quantum potest quisque nitatur, ne ille non magno desiderio tenebitur virium. Olympiae per stadium ingressus esse Milo

consul Manius Glabrio.[39] But nonetheless, as you can plainly see, old age has not unnerved or shattered me. Neither the Senate nor the popular assembly nor my friends nor my followers nor my guests find my strength lacking. I give no credit to that ancient and much-praised proverb that advises us to become old early if we want to be old long. Personally, I would rather be old for a shorter time than to be old too soon. Therefore, I have never refused an appointment with anyone who wanted to meet with me.

33. It's true that I don't have the strength of either of you—but then again neither of you has the strength of the centurion Titus Pontius.[40] Does that mean that he is a better person than you? Let each use properly whatever strengths he has and strive to use them well. If he does this, he will never find

dicitur, cum umeris sustineret bovem: utrum igitur has corporis an Pythagorae tibi malis vires ingeni dari? Denique isto bono utare dum adsit, cum absit ne requiras; nisi forte adulescentes pueritiam, paululum aetate progressi adulescentiam debent requirere. Cursus est certus aetatis, et una via naturae eaque simplex; suaque cuique parti aetatis tempestivitas est data, ut et infirmitas puerorum, et ferocitas iuvenum, et gravitas iam constantis aetatis, et senectutis maturitas, naturale quiddam habeat quod suo tempore percipi debeat.

34. Audire te arbitror, Scipio, hospes tuus avitus Masinissa quae faciat hodie nonaginta natus annos; cum ingressus iter pedibus sit,

himself lacking. They say that Milo walked the length of the Olympic stadium carrying an ox on his shoulders. But what would you prefer to be given, the physical strength of Milo or the mental power of Pythagoras? In short, enjoy the blessing of bodily strength while you have it, but don't mourn when it passes away, any more than a young man should lament the end of boyhood or a mature man the passing of youth. The course of life cannot change. Nature has but a single path and you travel it only once. Each stage of life has its own appropriate qualities—weakness in childhood, boldness in youth, seriousness in middle age, and maturity in old age. These are fruits that must be harvested in due season.

34. I expect, Scipio, that you sometimes hear news about your grandfather's friend and host Masinissa, who is now ninety years

in equum omnino non ascendere, cum autem equo, ex equo non descendere; nullo imbri, nullo frigore adduci ut capite operto sit, summam esse in eo siccitatem corporis; itaque omnia exsequi regis officia et munera. Potest igitur exercitatio et temperantia etiam in senectute conservare aliquid pristini roboris.

Non sunt in senectute vires? Ne postulantur quidem vires a senectute. Ergo et legibus et institutis vacat aetas nostra muneribus eis quae non possunt sine viribus sustineri, itaque non modo quod non possumus, sed ne quantum possumus quidem cogimur.

35. At multi ita sunt imbecilli senes, ut nullum offici aut omnino vitae munus

old.[41] Once he begins a journey by foot, he never mounts a horse. Likewise, when he sets out on horseback he never dismounts. He goes bareheaded even in the rain and cold. He is in such good condition that he still carries out all his royal duties and functions in person. This shows how a man who practices exercise and self-control can preserve some of his original vigor even when he grows old.

But let us assume that old age makes us feeble—what does it matter? No one expects older people to be physically strong in any case. That is why both law and custom exempt men my age from public duties requiring bodily strength. We aren't expected to perform tasks we cannot do nor even those things we can do.

35. Of course, many older people truly are in poor health, so that they are unable

exsequi possint. At id quidem non pro-
prium senectutis vitium est, sed commune
valetudinis. Quam fuit imbecillus Publius
Africani filius, is qui te adoptavit, quam
tenui aut nulla potius valetudine! Quod ni
ita fuisset, alterum illud exstitisset lumen
civitatis; ad paternam enim magnitudinem
animi doctrina uberior accesserat. Quid
mirium igitur in senibus, si infirmi sint
aliquando, cum id ne adulescentes quidem
effugere possint? Resistendum, Laeli et
Scipio, senectuti est, eiusque vitia diligentia
compensanda sunt, pugnandum tamquam
contra morbum, sic contra senectutem.

36. Habenda ratio valetudinis, utendum
exercitationibus modicis, tantum cibi et

to carry out normal duties or indeed any tasks that life demands. However, this inability is not a factor of old age but a characteristic of poor health in general. Remember, Scipio, the weakness of your adoptive father, the son of Publius Africanus.[42] He had poor health—or rather no health at all. Had it not been so, he would have been the second glory of our country, for in addition to his father's courage he possessed more abundant learning. Therefore, since even the young cannot escape infirmity, why should we marvel that old people sometimes lack physical strength?

We must fight, my dear Laelius and Scipio, against old age. We must compensate for its drawbacks by constant care and attend to its defects as if it were a disease.

36. We can do this by following a plan of healthy living, exercising in moderation,

potionis adhibendum ut reficiantur vires, non opprimantur. Nec vero corpori solum subveniendum est, sed menti atque animo multo magis; nam haec quoque, nisi tamquam lumini oleum instilles, exstinguuntur senectute; et corpora quidem exercitationum defatigatione ingravescunt, animi autem exercendo levantur. Nam quos ait Caecilius 'comicos stultos senes', hos significat credulos obliviosos dissolutos, quae vitia sunt non senectutis, sed inertis ignavae somniculosae senectutis. Ut petulantia, ut libido magis est adulescentium quam senum, nec tamen omnium adulescentium sed non proborum, sic ista senilis stultitia quae deliratio appellari solet, senum levium est, non omnium.

and eating and drinking just enough to restore our bodies without overburdening
them. And as much as we should care for
our bodies, we should pay even more attention to our minds and spirits. For they,
like lamps of oil, will grow dim with time if
not replenished. And even though physical
exercise may tire the body, mental activity
makes the mind sharper. When the playwright Caecilius speaks of "old fools of the
comic stage," he means men who are gull-
ible, forgetful, and lazy—qualities that be-
long not to old age in general but only to
those who have allowed themselves to become drowsy, sluggish, and inert. Wanton-
ness and lust are more common in the young
than in the old, yet they are not found in
all youth, just those of poor character. So
too the senile silliness we call "dotage" is

37. Quattuor robustos filios, quinque fil-
ias, tantam domum, tantas clientelas, Appius regebat et caecus et senex; intentum
enim animum tamquam arcum habebat, nec
languescens succumbebat senectuti. Tenebat non modo auctoritatem, sed etiam im-
perium in suos: metuebant servi, vereban-
tur liberi, carum omnes habebant; vigebat
in illa domo mos patrius et disciplina.

38. Ita enim senectus honesta est, si se
ipsa defendit, si ius suum retinet, si nemini
emancipata est, si usque ad ultimum spiritum dominatur in suos. Ut enim adules-
centem in quo est senile aliquid, sic senem
in quo est aliquid adulescentis probo; quod
qui sequitur corpore senex esse poterit,
animo numquam erit. Septimus mihi liber

characteristic not of all old people but only those who are weak in spirit and will.

37. Appius Claudius was old and blind, yet he led a household of four vigorous sons, five daughters, numerous servants, and many dependents. He did not lazily succumb to old age but kept his mind taut as a bow. He didn't direct his household as much as he ruled over it. His slaves feared him, his children venerated him, and all held him dear. The traditions and discipline of his forefathers flourished in his home.

38. For old age is respected only if it defends itself, maintains its rights, submits to no one, and rules over its domain until its last breath. Just as I approve of a young man with a touch of age about him, I applaud an old man who maintains some flavor of his youth. Such a person may grow old in body but never in spirit.

Originum est in manibus; omnia antiquitatis monumenta colligo, causarum illustrium quascumque defendi nunc cum maxime conficio orationes, ius augurium, pontificium civile tracto; multumque etiam Graecis litteris utor, Pythagoreorumque more, exercendae memoriae gratia, quid quoque die dixerim, audierim egerim commemoro vesperi. Hae sunt exercitationes ingeni, haec curricula mentis; in his desudans atque elaborans corporis vires non magnopere desidero. Adsum amicis, venio in senatum frequens; ultroque adfero res multum et diu cogitatas, easque tueor animi, non corporis viribus. Quas si exsequi nequirem, tamen me lectulus meus oblectaret, ea ipsa cogitantem quae iam agere non possem. Sed ut possim facit acta vita; semper enim in his studiis laboribusque viventi, non intellegitur

I am now working on the seventh book of my *Origins* and collecting all the records of our earliest history, as well as editing the speeches I delivered in famous cases.[43] I am investigating augural, priestly, and civil law. I also devote much of my time to the study of Greek literature. And to exercise my memory, I follow the practice of the Pythagoreans and each evening go over everything I have said, heard, or done during the day. These are my mental gymnastics, the racecourses of my mind. And although I sweat and toil with them, I don't greatly miss my former bodily strength. I also provide legal advice to my friends and frequently attend meetings of the Senate, where I propose topics for discussion and argue my opinion after pondering the issues long and hard.

quando obrepat senectus; ita sensim sine sensu aetas senescit, nec subito frangitur, sed diuturnitate exstinguitur.

39. Sequitur tertia vituperatio senectutis, quod eam carere dicunt voluptatibus. O praeclarum munus aetatis, siquidem id aufert a nobis quod est in adulescentia vitiosissimum! Accipite enim, optimi adulescentes,

All this I do not with the strength of my body but with the force of my mind. Even if the effort of doing these things were more than I could manage, I could still lie on my reading couch and think about the activities that were now beyond me. But the fact that I can do them I owe to my vigorous life. For a man who has been engaged in studies and activities his whole life does not notice old age creeping up on him. Instead, he gradually and effortlessly slips into his final years, not overcome suddenly but extinguished over a long period.

The Pleasures of Age

39. We come now to the third objection to growing older—that the pleasures of the flesh fade away. But if this is true, I say it is indeed a glorious gift that age frees us from youth's most destructive failing.

veterem orationem Archytae Tarentini, magni in primis et praeclari viri, quae mihi tradita est cum essem adulescens Tarenti cum Quinto Maximo. Nullam capitaliorem pestem quam voluptatem corporis hominibus dicebat a natura datam, cuius voluptatis avidae libidines temere et ecfrenate ad potiendum incitarentur.

40. Hinc patriae proditiones, hinc rerum publicarum eversiones, hinc cum hostibus clandestina colloquia nasci; nullum denique scelus, nullum malum facinus esse, ad quod suscipiendum non libido voluptatis impelleret; stupra vero et adulteria et omne tale flagitium nullis excitari aliis illecebris nisi voluptatis; cumque homini sive natura sive quis deus nihil mente praestabilius dedisset, huic divino muneri ac dono nihil tam esse inimicum quam voluptatem.

Now listen, my most noble young friends, to the ancient words of that excellent and most distinguished man, Archytas of Tarentum, repeated to me when I was serving as a young soldier in that very city with Quintus Maximus:[44] He said the most fatal curse given to men by nature is sexual desire. From it spring passions of uncontrollable and reckless lust seeking gratification.

40. From it come secret plotting with enemies, betrayals of one's country, and the overthrow of governments. Indeed, there is no evil act, no unscrupulous deed that a man driven by lust will not perform. Uncontrolled sensuality will drive men to rape, adultery, and every other sexual outrage. And since nature—or perhaps some god— has given men no finer gift than human intelligence, this divine endowment has no greater foe than naked sensuality.

41. Nec enim libidine dominante temperantiae locum esse, neque omnino in voluptatis regno virtutem posse consistere. Quod quo magis intellegi posset, fingere animo iubebat tanta incitatum aliquem voluptate corporis quanta percipi posset maxima; nemini censebat fore dubium, quin tamdiu dum ita gauderet, nihil agitare mente, nihil ratione, nihil cogitatione consequi posset. Quocirca nihil esse tam detestabile tamque pestiferum quam voluptatem, siquidem ea cum maior esset atque longinquior, omne animi lumen exstingueret. Haec cum Gaio Pontio Samnite, patre eius a quo Caudino proelio Sp. Postumius T. Veturius consules superati sunt, locutum Archytam, Nearchus Tarentinus hospes noster, qui in amicitia populi Romani permanserat, se a maioribus natu accepisse dicebat; cum quidem ei sermoni interfuisset

41. Where lust rules, there is no place for self-control. And in the kingdom of self-indulgence, there is no room for decent behavior.

"Imagine," Archytas continued, to make his meaning clearer, "a person enjoying the most exquisite sensual pleasure possible. No one would doubt that a man in that state is incapable of using his mind in any rational or reasonable way. Therefore, nothing is more detestable or pernicious than sensual pleasure. If a person indulges in it too much and too long, it plunges the soul into utter darkness."

Nearchus, a steadfast friend of Rome who was my host at Tarentum, told me that according to tradition Archytas spoke these words to Gaius Pontius the Samnite, father of the man who defeated the consuls Spurius Postumius and Titus Veturius at the

Plato Atheniensis, quem Tarentum venisse
L. Camillo Ap. Claudio consulibus reperio.

42. Quorsus hoc? Ut intellegeretis, si voluptatem aspernari ratione et sapientia non
possumus, magnam habendam esse senectuti gratiam, quae efficeret, ut id non liberet
quod non operteret. Impedit enim consilium voluptas, rationi inimica est, mentis
ut ita dicam, praestringit oculos, nec habet
ullum cum virtute commercium. Invitus
feci ut fortissimi viri Titi Flaminini fratrem
Lucium Flamininum e senatu eicerem, septem annis postquam consul fuisset, sed
notandam putavi libidinem: ille enim cum
esset consul in Gallia, exoratus in convivio
a scorto est, ut securi feriret aliquem eorum

Caudine Forks.[45] Nearchus added that Plato the Athenian was present and heard him utter these words. And indeed I have investigated this and found that Plato did come to Tarentum when Lucius Camillus and Appius Claudius were consuls.[46]

42. So why have I quoted Archytas? To make you see that if reason and wisdom aren't enough to make us reject lustful desires, then we should be grateful that old age takes away the craving to do what is wrong. For such feelings cloud our judgment, are at war with reason, and, if I may say so, blind the eyes of the mind and allow no room for living a good life.

It was an unpleasant duty I performed when I had to eject from the Senate a man who had been consul seven years earlier—Lucius Flamininus, the brother of that most worthy Titus Flamininus.[47] But I believed

qui in vinculis essent, damnati rei capitalis. Hic Tito fratre suo censore (qui proximus ante me fuerat) elapsus est, mihi vero et Flacco neutiquam probari potuit tam flagitiosa et tam perdita libido, quae cum probro privato coniungeret imperi dedecus.

43. Saepe audivi a maioribus natu, qui se porro pueros a senibus audisse dicebant, mirari solitum Gaium Fabricium, quod cum apud regem Pyrrhum legatus esset, audisset a Thessalo Cinea esse quendam Athenis qui se sapientem profiteretur, eumque dicere omnia quae faceremus ad voluptatem esse referenda; quod ex eo audientis, Manium Curium et Tiberium Coruncanium optare

his shameful lust had demanded this action. For when he was a consul in Gaul, he executed, at the request of a prostitute during a banquet, some man imprisoned for a capital offense. During the time when his brother, my immediate predecessor, had been censor, Lucius had escaped punishment. But Flaccus and I could not permit such flagrant and indecent passion to go unanswered, especially since his scandalous crime against a private individual had dishonored Rome.

43. I often heard from elders—who said they heard it from old men when they were boys—that Gaius Fabricius used to marvel at a story told to him (while he was on a mission to King Pyrrhus) by Cineas of Thessaly.[48] Cineas said that there was an Athenian professing to be wise who claimed that everything we do should be judged by how much pleasure it gives us.[49] Now, when

solitos ut id Samnitibus ipsique Pyrrho
persuaderetur, quod facilius vinci possent
cum se voluptatibus dedissent. Vixerat
Manius Curius cum Publio Decio, qui
quinquennio ante eum consulem se pro re
publica quarto consulatu devoverat; norat
eundem Fabricius, norat Coruncanius; qui
cum ex sua vita, tum ex eius, quem dico
Deci facto, iudicabant esse profecto aliquid natura pulchrum atque praeclarum,
quod sua sponte peteretur, quodque spreta
et contempta voluptate optimus quisque
sequeretur.

44. Quorsus igitur tam multa de voluptate? Quia non modo vituperatio nulla

Manius Curius and Tiberius Coruncanius heard this from Fabricius, they said they hoped that the Samnites and Pyrrhus himself would adopt his teaching, since it's easier to conquer people who surrender to pleasure. Manius Curius had been a good friend of Publius Decius, who, while consul for the fourth time (and five years before Curius himself was consul), had sacrificed his life for his country.[50] Fabricius and Coruncanius knew him as well. They were firmly convinced, as shown by the lives they led and especially by Decius's final act, that certain goals in life are naturally fine and noble and should be sought for their own sake. They believed that every decent person should pursue these goals and reject self-indulgence as contemptible.

44. Why am I talking so much about pleasure? Because the fact that old age feels

sed etiam summa laus senectutis est, quod ea voluptates nullas magnopere desiderat. Caret epulis extructisque mensis et frequentibus poculis; caret ergo etiam vinulentia et cruditate et insomniis. Sed si aliquid dandum est voluptati (quoniam eius blanditiis non facile resistimus; divine enim Plato escam malorum appellat voluptatam, quod ea videlicet homines capiantur ut pisces), quamquam immoderatis epulis caret senectus, modicis tamen coviviis delectari potest. Gaium Duellium Marci filium, qui Poenos classe primus devicerat, redeuntem a cena senem saepe videbam puer; delectabatur cereo funali et tibicine, quae sibi nullo exemplo privatus sumpserat; tantum licentiae dabat gloria.

little desire for sensual delights is not only no cause for reproach but indeed a reason to praise it highly. Old age has no extravagant banquets, no tables piled high, no wine cups filled again and again, but it also has no drunkenness, no indigestion, and no sleepless nights!

However, if we must make some concession to pleasure, since its allurement is hard to resist—"the bait of evil" Plato brilliantly calls it, men caught in its net like fish[51]—then I admit we should allow old age, though it lacks excessive feasts, the delights of more moderate dinners. When I was a child I often saw old Gaius Duilius, son of Marcus, who first defeated the Carthaginians in a naval battle, walking home from dinner parties.[52] He always loved being escorted on these little journeys by torchbearers and a flute player. No private citizen had

45. Sed quid ego alios? Ad me ipsum iam revertar. Primum habui semper sodalis; sodalitates autem me quaestore constitutae sunt sacris Idaeis Magnae Matris acceptis. Epulabar igitur cum sodalibus, omnino modice, sed erat quidam fervor aetatis; qua progrediente omnia fiunt in dies mitiora; neque enim ipsorum conviviorum delecta- tionem voluptatibus corporis magis quam coetu amicorum et sermonibus metiebar. Bene enim maiores accubitionem epularem amicorum, quia vitae coniunctionem habe- ret, convivium nominaverunt, melius quam Graeci, qui hoc idem tum compotationem tum concenationem vocant, ut quod in eo genere minimum est, id maxime probare videantur.

behaved in such a way previously, but his glorious reputation gave him license.

45. But why do I speak of others? Let me return now to myself. To begin with, I have always had my club companions. It was during my quaestorship that clubs in honor of the Great Mother and her Idaean worship were introduced at Rome.[53] I used to regularly dine with these companions in a modest fashion, yet with a certain fervor of youth most appropriate then, though it diminishes as time goes by. But it wasn't the gastronomic delights that appealed to me even then as much as the pleasure of meeting and conversing with my friends. The word our ancestors used for a meal with friends was *convivium*—a "living together"—because it describes the essence of a social gathering. It's a much richer description of the experience than the Greek

46. Ego vero propter sermonis delecta-
tionem tempestivis quoque conviviis delector, nec cum aequalibus solum, qui pauci
admodum restant, sed cum vestra etiam
aetate atque vobiscum; habeoque senectuti
magnam gratiam, quae mihi sermonis avid-
itatem auxit, potionis et cibi sustulit. Quod
si quem etiam ista delectant (ne omnino
bellum indixisse videar voluptati, cuius est
fortasse quidam naturalis modus), non intellego ne in istis quidem ipsis voluptatibus
carere sensu senectutem. Me vero et magis-
teria delectant a maioribus instituta, et is
sermo qui more maiorum a summo adhibe-
tur in poculo, et pocula sicut in Symposio

terms "drinking together" or "eating to-gether," which emphasize what is least im-portant in these gatherings rather than what is most valuable.[54]

46. Personally, because I love conversa-tion, I even enjoy dinner parties that start early in the day. At these gatherings, I talk not only with my contemporaries—very few of whom remain—but also with you and your young friends. I am so grateful to old age for increasing my delight in conver-sation while lessening my desire for food and drink. But if any of my older friends enjoy these things—and let no one think that I have declared war on pleasure since a certain amount of it has perhaps been justi-fied by nature—then let me say that I know no reason old age should be lacking in such gratification.

Xenophontis est, minuta atque rorantia, et refrigeratio aestate et vicissim aut sol aut ignis hibernus. Quae quidem etiam in Sabinis persequi soleo, conviviumque vicinorum cotidie compleo, quod ad multam noctem quam maxime possumus vario sermone producimus.

47. At non est voluptatum tanta quasi titillatio in senibus. Credo, sed ne desideratio quidem; nihil autem est molestum, quod non desideres. Bene Sophocles, cum ex eo quidem iam adfecto aetate quaereret, utereturne rebus veneriis, 'Di meliora!' inquit, 'libenter vero istinc sicut ab domino agresti

I very much appreciate our ancestral custom of appointing a banquet leader for social gatherings and starting the conversation at the head of the table when the wine comes in. I also like cups as described in Xenophon's *Symposium*, small and filled as if with dew, cool in the summer and warmed in winter by sunshine or fire.[55] Even when I'm among the rustic Sabines I frequent such gatherings. And when at home with my neighbors, I join them every day for a meal where we talk as long into the night as we can about all sorts of things.

47. But of course some people will point out that the old aren't as able as the young to have their senses tickled. That's true, but they don't yearn for it either, and nothing troubles you if you don't desire it. Sophocles, when he was already an old man, gave a great answer to someone who asked if he

ac furioso profugi.' Cupidis enim rerum ta-
lium odiosum fortasse et molestum est carere, satiatis vero et expletis iucundius est
carere quam frui; quamquam non caret is
qui non desiderat, ergo hoc non desiderare
dico esse iucundius.

48. Quod si istis ipsis voluptatibus bona
aetas fruitur libentius, primum parvulis
fruitur rebus ut diximus, deinde eis quibus
senectus etiamsi non abunde potitur, non
omnino caret. Ut Turpione Ambivio magis
delectatur qui in prima cavea spectat, delectatur tamen etiam qui in ultima, sic
adulescentia voluptates propter intuens
magis fortasse laetatur, sed delectatur etiam

still enjoyed sex. "Good gods, no!" he said. "I have gladly escaped that cruel and savage master."[56]

For those who yearn for such things, not to have them is perhaps troublesome and annoying. But if you've had your fill of sex and have satisfied all such desires, then to lack them is better than to possess them. If you don't long for something, you don't miss it. That's why I say the absence of desire is quite pleasant.

48. But granting that young people enjoy the pleasures of the flesh more than the old, I need to make two points. First, as I've said, these kinds of pleasures matter little. Second, even though old age doesn't provide these delights in abundance, it doesn't lack them completely. Just as Ambivius Turpio entertained the audience at the front of the theater more than those in the rear

senectus procul eas spectans tantum quantum sat est.

49. At illi quanti est, animum tamquam
emeritis stipendiis libidinis, ambitionis,
contentionis, inimicitiarum, cupiditatum
omnium, secum esse secumque ut dicitur
vivere! Si vero habet aliquod tamquam pab-
ulum studi atque doctrinae, nihil est otiosa
senectute iucundius. Videbamus in studio
dimetiendi paene caeli atque terrae Gaium
Galum, familiarem patris tui, Scipio. Quotiens illum lux, noctu aliquid describere in-
gressum, quotiens nox oppressit cum mane
coepisset! Quam delectabat eum defectiones
solis et lunae multo ante nobis praedicere!

seats, still he gave those in back a good show as well.[57] In the same way, young people may enjoy sex more than the old, but the elderly still can appreciate it sufficiently by looking on such pleasures from a distance.

49. How wonderful it is for the soul when—after so many struggles with lust, ambition, strife, quarreling, and other passions—these battles are at last ended and it can return, as they say, to live within itself. There is no greater satisfaction to be had in life than a leisurely old age devoted to knowledge and learning. I used to see, Scipio, your father's friend Gaius Gallus measuring, you might say, the whole of the heavens and the earth. How often the morning sun surprised him as he worked on some chart he had begun the previous night. And how often night overtook him at a task he had begun at dawn. How he

50. Quid in levioribus studiis, sed tamen acutis, quam gaudebat Bello suo Punico Naevius, quam Truculento Plautus, quam Pseudolo? Vidi etiam senem Livium, qui cum sex aniis antequam ego natus sum fabulam docuisset Centone Tuditanoque consulibus, usque ad adulescentiam meam processit aetate. Quid de Publi Licini Crassi et pontifici et civilis iuris studio loquar, aut de huius Publi Scipionis qui his paucis diebus pontifex maximus factus est? Atque eos omnes quos commemoravi, his studiis flagrantis senes vidimus; Marcum vero Cethegum, quem recte 'Suadae medullam' dixit Ennius, quanto studio exerceri in dicendo videbamus etiam senem! Quae sunt igitur epularum aut ludorum aut scortorum voluptates cum his voluptatibus comparandae?

delighted in telling us about eclipses of the sun and moon before they happened!

50. And let's not forget others who engaged in easier but no less demanding work. How Naevius delighted in his *Punic War*, as did Plautus in *The Savage* and *The Cheat*.[58] I myself saw Livius Andronicus when he was an old man.[59] He brought out a play six years before I was born—when Cento and Tuditanus were consuls—yet he continued to live until I was a young man.[60] I don't need to mention again the example of Publius Licinius Crassus, who was active in religious and civic law, or bring up Publius Scipio, who was elected chief priest just a few days ago.[61] Yet I have seen all these men still enthusiastic in their callings after they grew old. There was also Marcus Cethegus, whom Ennius rightly described as "the marrow of persuasion."[62] I myself saw

Atque haec quidem studia doctrinae quae quidem prudentibus et bene institutis pariter cum aetate crescunt, ut honestum illud Solonis sit, quod ait versiculo quodam ut ante dixi, senescere se multa in dies addiscentem, qua voluptate animi nulla certe potest esse maior.

51. Venio nunc ad voluptates agricolarum, quibus ego incredibiliter delector; quae nec ulla impediuntur senectute, et mihi ad sapientis vitam proxime videntur accedere. Habent enim rationem cum terra, quae numquam recusat impendium, nec umquam

him speak with exuberance even though he was an old man.

How can anyone compare the pleasures of banquets or games or brothels to what these men enjoyed? They had a passion for learning, a passion that in sensible and educated people advances as the years go by. So there is truth in Solon's verse I quoted in which he said that as he grew older he learned more and more every day. Surely there can be no greater pleasure than the pleasure of the mind.

The Joys of Farming

51. Now, speaking of pleasures, let me tell you about farming, which brings me a great deal of personal joy. The pleasures of growing things are not at all diminished by age and they seem to me most suitable for the life of a wise person. The joys of farming

sine usura reddit quod accepit, sed alias minore, plerumque maiore cum faenore. Quamquam me quidem non fructus modo, sed etiam ipsius terrae vis ac natura delectat; quae cum gremio mollito ac subacto sparsum semen excepit, primum id occaecatum cohibet, ex quo occatio quae hoc efficit nominata est, dein tepefactum vapore et compressu suo diffundit et elicit herbescentem ex eo viriditatem; quae nixa fibris stirpium sensim adulescit, culmoque erecta geniculato vaginis iam quasi pubescens includitur; ex quibus cum emersit, fundit frugem spici ordine exstructam, et contra avium minorum morsus munitur vallo aristarum.

are like a bank account with the earth itself, which never refuses to honor a withdrawal and always returns the principal with interest, though sometimes only a little yet at other times a great deal.

What delights me are not only the fruits of the land but the power and nature of the earth itself. It receives the scattered seed in its softened and ready womb, and for a time the seed remains hidden—*occaecatum* in Latin, hence our word *occatio*.[63] Then warmed by the moist heat of its embrace, the seed expands and brings forth a green and flourishing blade. With the support of its fibrous roots, it grows and matures until at last it stands erect on its jointed stalk. Now within its sheath it has reached its adolescent stage so that finally it bursts forth and an ear of grain comes into the light with

52. Quid ego vitium ortus satus incrementa commemorem? Satiari delectatione non possum (ut meae senectutis requiem oblectamentumque noscatis): omitto enim vim ipsam omnium quae generantur e terra, quae e fici tantulo grano aut ex acini vinaceo aut ex ceterarum frugum aut stirpium minutissimis seminibus tantos truncos ramosque procreet; malleoli plantae sarmenta viviradices propagines, nonne ea efficiunt ut quemvis cum admiratione delectent? Vitis quidem, quae natura caduca est et nisi fulta est fertur ad terram, eadem ut se erigat claviculis suis quicquid est nacta complectitur; quam serpentem multiplici lapsu et erratico, ferro amputans coercet ars agricolarum, ne silvescat sarmentis et in omnes partes nimia fundatur.

ordered rows and a palisade of spikes as protection against nibbling by small birds.

52. I really shouldn't mention the vine—its beginnings, cultivation, and growth. But I must tell you that tending vines is the rejuvenation and delight of my old age. I simply can't get enough of it. I won't dwell here on the inherent force of all things that are generated from the earth—how from a tiny fig seed or grape stone or from the smallest seeds of any fruit or plant mighty trunks and branches grow. Just consider the planting of shoots, the twigs, the cuttings, the sprouts—isn't it enough to fill anyone with admiration? Vines naturally want to droop on the earth, but prop them up and they will raise their tendrils like hands to the sky. They twist and turn in every course until the farmer's pruning knife checks them lest they turn to wood and spread too abundantly.

53. Itaque ineunte vere in eis quae relicta est exsistit tamquam ad articulos sarmentorum, ea quae gemma dicitur; ex qua oriens uva se ostendit, quae et suco terrae et calore solis augescens, primo est peracerba gustatu, deinde maturata dulcescit, vestitaque pampinis nec modico tepore caret et nimios solis defendit ardores. Qua quid potest esse cum fructu laetius, tum aspectu pulchrius? Cuius quidem non utilitas me solum ut ante dixi, sed etiam cultura et natura ipsa delectat—adminiculorum ordines, capitum iugatio, religatio et propagatio vitium, sarmentorum ea quam dixi aliorum amputatio, aliorum immissio. Quid ego irrigationes, quid fossiones agri repastinationesque proferam, quibus fit multo terra fecundior?

53. With the coming of spring, the branches left on a vine at every joint put forth a bud, which in turn become swelling grapes. These are bitter at first, but soon the moisture of the earth and heat of the sun turn them sweet as they ripen, wrapped by leaves to provide moderate warmth and keep away the burning rays of the sun. What indeed could be more alluring to the taste or pleasing to the eye?

Now, it isn't simply the usefulness of the vine that delights me, as I said before, but its cultivation and very nature. Just consider the rows of stakes, the vine tops joined to trellises, the tying up of the branches, the extending of the vines, and the pruning of some branches, as I said, while others are left to grow freely.

Why should I now mention irrigation, ditching, and the hoeing of the ground that

54. Quid de utilitate loquar stercorandi? Dixi in eo libro quem de rebus rusticis scripsi; de qua doctus Hesiodus ne verbum quidem fecit, cum de cultura agri scriberet; at Homerus, qui multis ut mihi videtur ante saeculis fuit, Laetam lenientem desiderium quod capiebat e filio, colentem agrum et eum stercorantem facit. Nec vero segetibus solum et pratis et vineis et arbustis res rusticae laetae sunt, sed hortis etiam et pomariis; tum pecudum pastu, apium examinibus, florum omnium varietate; nec consitiones modo delectant, sed etiam insitiones, quibus nihil invenit agri cultura sollertius.

55. Possum persequi permulta oblectamenta rerum rusticarum, sed ea ipsa quae

makes the land more productive? Why should I discuss here the usefulness of manure? You can read all about this in my book on agriculture.[64]

54. Even the learned Hesiod says nothing of this matter, although he wrote on agriculture.[65] But Homer, who I believe lived many generations earlier, does mention Odysseus's father Laertes soothed his sorrow over his absent son by tilling his land and manuring it too.[66]

The farmer also enjoys his fields, meadows, vineyards, and woodlands, his gardens and orchards, cattle pastures, swarming bees, and all manner of flowers. Planting too is a delight, and grafting as well, a most ingenious operation of agriculture.

55. I could go on and on about the charms of farming, though I have said too much

dixi sentio fuisse longiora; ignoscetis autem, nam et studio rerum rusticarum provectus sum, et senectus est natura loquacior—ne ab omnibus eam vitiis videar vindicare. Ergo in hac vita Manius Curius, cum de Samnitibus, de Sabinis, de Pyrrho triumphasset, consumpsit extremum tempus aetatis; cuius quidem ego villam contemplans—abest enim non longe a me—admirari satis non possum vel hominis ipsius continentiam vel temporum disciplinam.

56. Curio ad focum sedenti magnum auri pondus Samnites cum attulissent, repudiati sunt; non enim aurum habere praeclarum sibi videri dixit, sed eis qui haberent aurum imperare. Poteratne tantus animus efficere non iucundam senctutem? Sed venio ad agricolas, ne a me ipso recedam: in agris erant

already. But do forgive me if I continue, for my enthusiasm for the rustic life carries me away. And besides, old age is naturally talkative—I don't want to excuse it of all its faults.

They say that Manius Curius spent the remainder of his life in farming after he had triumphed over the Samnites, Sabines, and Pyrrhus. And as I gaze at his country house, not far from my own, I cannot admire enough the frugality of the man or the disciplined spirit of his times.

56. Once, while he was sitting by his fireside, some Samnites brought him a large gift of gold. But he rejected this, saying that it seemed to him less glorious to possess gold than to rule over those who have it. A man with such a great soul must have found much happiness in old age.

tum senatores, id est senes, siquidem aranti
Lucio Quinctio Cincinnato nuntiatum est
eum dictatorem esse factum; cuius dictato-
ris iussu magister equitum Gaius Servilius
Ahala Spurium Maelium regnum appeten-
tem occupatum interemit. A villa in senatum arcessebatur et Curius et ceteri senes,
ex quo qui eos arcessebant viatores nominati sunt. Num igitur horum senectus mis-
erabilis fuit, qui se agri cultione oblecta-
bant? Mea quidem sententia haud scio an
nulla beatior possit esse: neque solum offi-
cio, quod hominum generi universo cultura
agrorum est salutaris, sed et delectatione
qua dixi, et saturitate copiaque rerum omnium quae ad victum hominum, ad cultum
etiam deorum pertinent; ut quoniam haec
quidem desiderant, in gratiam iam cum voluptate redeamus. Semper enim boni assi-
duique domini referta cella vinaria, olearia,

But lest I wander away from my subject, let me return to farmers. In former days, senators (that is, *senes*, "elders") were farmers, if indeed the story is true that Lucius Quinctius Cincinnatus was at his plough when they called him to be dictator. By the order of Cincinnatus, Gaius Servilius Ahala, his master of the horse, seized Spurius Maelius and put him to death for attempting to make himself king.[67] It was from their distant farmhouses that Curius and other elders were summoned to the Senate. That is why the messengers sent to bring them were called *viatores* — "travelers."

Surely men like these who delighted in working the land could not have been unhappy when they grew old? I personally believe that no life can be happier than that of a farmer, not only because of the service provided that benefits the entire human race,

etiam penaria est, villaque tota locuples est, abundat porco haedo agno gallina lacte caseo melle. Iam hortum ipsi agricolae succidiam alteram appellant; conditiora facit haec supervacaneis etiam operis aucupium atque venatio.

57. Quid de pratorum viriditate aut arborum ordinibus aut vinearum olivetorumve specie plura dicamus? Brevi praecidam: agro

but because of the pleasures I mentioned earlier and the abundance of all things needed for worship of the gods and the sustenance of humanity.

Seeing that some people are very concerned with material goods, I hope this talk of abundance will return me to their good graces. For the farmer who looks ahead and works hard always has his storage rooms and cellars full of wine, oil, and provisions. His whole farm is filled with an air of plenty with rooms of abundant pork, goat meat, lamb, poultry, milk, cheese, and honey. Then there is the farmer's own garden, which he calls his "second leg of pork." What spare time he has is sweetened with activities such as bird-catching and hunting.

57. Why should I speak at length about the greenness of meadows, the ordered rows of trees, the glory of vineyards and olive

bene culto nihil potest esse nec usu uberius
nec specie ornatius; ad quem fruendum
non modo non retardat verum etiam invitat
atque adlectat senectus. Ubi enim potest
illa aetas aut calescere vel apricatione melius vel igni, aut vicissim umbris aquisve
refrigerari salubrius?

58. Sibi habeant igitur arma, sibi equos,
sibi hastas, sibi clavam et pilam, sibi vena-
tiones atque cursus, nobis senibus ex lusion-
ibus multis talos relinquant et tesseras—id
ipsum ut libebit, quoniam sine eis beata
esse senectus potest.

59. Multas ad res perutiles Xenophontis
libri sunt, quos legite quaeso studiose, ut
facitis. Quam copiose ab eo agricultura

groves? Instead, I will be brief. Nothing can be more abundantly useful or beautiful than a well-kept farm. Not only does old age not impede the enjoyment of such a farm, but it actually invites and increases its enjoyment. For where else in the world can an old man better find warmth from the sunshine or the hearth? Or where else in the summertime can he more healthfully cool himself with shade or running water?

58. Let others have their weapons, their horses, their spears and fencing foils, their balls, their swimming contests and foot races. Just leave old men like me our dice and knucklebones. Or take away those too if you want. Old age can be happy without them.

59. The writings of Xenophon are very informative on many subjects and I recommend you read them carefully, as I know

laudatur in eo libro qui est de tuenda re
familiari, qui Oeconomicus inscribitur!
Atque ut intellegatis nihil ei tam regale videri quam studium agri colendi, Socrates in
eo libro loquitur cum Critobulo, Cyrum
minorem, Persarum regem praestantem in-
genio atque imperi gloria, cum Lysander
Lacedaemonius, vir summae virtutis, venisset ad eum Sardis eique dona a sociis adtu-
lisset, et ceteris in rebus communem erga
Lysandrum atque humanum fuisse, et ei
quendam consaeptum agrum diligenter con-
situm ostendisse; cum autem admiraretur
Lysander et proceritates arborum et derec-
tos in quincuncem ordines et humum sub-
actam atque puram et suavitatem odorum
qui adflarentur e floribus, tum eum dixisse
mirari se non modo diligentiam sed etiam
sollertiam eius a quo essent illa dimensa atque
discripta; et Cyrum respondisse: 'Atqui ego

you already do. How greatly he praises agriculture in his book on estate management. To show you that Xenophon regarded agriculture as the most regal of pursuits, let me tell you a story from his book which he has Socrates relate in a conversation with Critobolus.[68]

Cyrus the Younger, a Persian prince known for his outstanding intelligence and the glory of his rule, was visited at Sardis by Lysander of Sparta, a man of the greatest virtue.[69] He had come to Sardis with gifts from their allies. Among the courtesies Cyrus extended to his guest was a tour of a carefully planted park. Lysander complimented the prince on the stately trees growing in patterns of five, the clean and well-tilled soil, and the sweet fragrance of the flowers. The Spartan then added that what impressed him was not only all the hard work that had

ista sum omnia dimensus, mei sunt ordines, mea descriptio, multae etiam istarum arborum mea manu sunt satae.' Tum Lysandrum, intuentem purpuram eius et nitorem corporis ornatumque Persicum multo auro multisque gemmis, dixisse; 'Recte vero te Cyre beatum ferunt, quoniam virtuti tuae fortuna coniuncta est.'

60. Hac igitur fortuna frui licet senibus, nec aetas impedit quominus et ceterarum rerum et in primis agri colendi studia teneamus usque ad ultimum tempus senectutis; Maecum quidem Valerium Corvinum accepimus ad centesimum annum perduxisse, cum esset acta iam aetate in agris eosque coleret; cuius inter primum et sextum

gone into the park but the ingenuity with which everything had been arranged. "It was I who planned it all," said Cyrus. "The rows are mine, the arrangement is mine, and I planted many of the trees with my own hands." After gazing at Cyrus's purple robes, the shining beauty of his body, and his Persian clothes decorated with gold and many precious stones, Lysander declared: "People are right to call you happy, Cyrus. Not only are you fortunate, but you are a virtuous man as well."

60. The good fortune of growing things is something every old person can enjoy. The cultivation of the soil is something we can pursue even to the end of our days. For example, we hear the story that Valerius Corvinus continued to work on his farm at an advanced age and so lived until he was a hundred years old.[70] His first and sixth

consulatum sex et quadraginta anni inter-
fuerunt; ita quantum spatium aetatis maiores
ad senectutis initium esse voluerunt, tantus
illi cursus honorum fuit; atque huius extrema aetas hoc beatior quam media, quod
auctoritatis habebat plus, laboris minus.
Apex est autem senectutis auctoritas.

61. Quanta fuit in Lucio Caecilio Me-
tello, quanta in Aulo Atilio Caiatino! in
quem illud elogium:

Hunc unum plurimae consentiunt gentes
populi primarium fuisse virum.

Notum est enim totum carmen incisum in
sepulcro; iure igitur gravis, cuius de laudi-
bus omnium esset fama consentiens. Quem
virum nuper Publium Crassum pontificem

consulships were forty-six years apart—in other words, the length of time our ancestors considered to be the span of a man's adult life until the start of old age. And the final part of his life was happier than what had come before since his influence was greater and he had fewer responsibilities.

The Honors of Old Age

61. The crowning glory of old age is respect. Great respect was given to Lucius Caecilius Metellus, as well as Aulus Atilius Caiatinus.[71] His epitaph reads:

> All the nations say this man
> was the noblest of his country.

But you know the whole epitaph since it is inscribed on his tomb. The universal acknowledgment of his fine qualities is

maximum, quem postea Marcum Lepidum
eodem sacerdotio praeditum, vidimus! Quid
de Paulo aut Africano loquar, aut ut iam
ante de Maximo? quorum non in sententia
solum sed etiam in nutu residebat auctoritas. Habet senectus honorata praesertim
tantam auctoritatem ut ea pluris sit quam
omnes adulescentiae voluptates.

62. Sed in omni oratione mementote eam
me senectutem laudare, quae fundamentis
adulescentiae constituta sit. Ex quo efficitur
id quod ego magno quondam cum assensu
omnium dixi, miseram esse senectutem quae
se oratione defenderet; non cani nec rugae
repente auctoritatem adripere possunt, sed
honeste acta superior aetas fructus capit
auctoritatis extremos.

testimony to his influence. We have seen in recent times the chief priest Publius Crassus and his successor Marcus Lepidus.[72] What men they were! And what should I say of Paullus and Africanus and Maximus, of whom I spoke earlier? These men exuded authority not only in their speech but in the mere nod of their head. Surely the respect given to old age crowned with public honors is more satisfying than all the sensual pleasures of youth.

62. But please bear in mind that throughout this whole discussion I am praising an old age that has its foundation well laid in youth. Thus it follows—as I once said with the approval of all who heard me—that an old age which must defend itself with words alone is unenviable. Wrinkles and gray hair cannot suddenly demand respect. Only when the earlier years of life have been

63. Haec enim ipsa sunt honorabilia quae videntur levia atque communia, salutari appeti decedi adsurgi deduci reduci consuli; quae et apud nos et in aliis civitatibus, ut quaeque optime morata est, ita diligentissime observantur. Lysandrum Lacedaemonium (cuius modo feci mentionem) dicere aiunt solitum, Lacedaemonem esse honestissimum domicilium senectutis: nusquam enim tantum tribuitur aetati, nusquam est senectus honoratior. Quin etiam memoriae proditum est, cum Athenis ludis quidam in theatrum grandis natu venisset magno consessu, locum nusquam ei datum a suis civibus; cum autem ad Lacedaemonios accessisset, qui legati cum essent certo in loco consederant, consurrexisse omnes illi dicuntur et senem sessum recepisse.

well spent does old age at last gather the fruits of admiration.

63. When that has finally happened, the signs of respect may at first seem unimportant or even trivial—morning visits, requests for meetings, people making way for you and rising when you approach, being escorted to and from the Forum, being asked for advice. We Romans scrupulously practice these civilities, as do all other decent nations.

It is reported that Lysander of Sparta, of whom I was just speaking, used to say that his city was the best place for the elderly, since his hometown treated old people with greater respect and deference than anywhere else. A story goes that once in Athens an old man went to a crowded theater to see a play, but not one of his countrymen offered him a seat. However, when he came to the section

64. Quibus cum a cuncto consessu plausus esset multiplex datus, dixisse ex eis quendam, Atheniensis scire quae recta essent, sed facere nolle. Multa in nostro collegio praeclara, sed hoc de quo agimus in primis, quod ut quisque aetate antecedit, ita sententiae principatum tenet, neque solum honore antecedentibus sed eis etiam qui cum imperio sunt, maiores natu augures anteponuntur. Quae sunt igitur voluptates corporis cum auctoritatis praemiis comparandae? Quibus qui splendide usi sunt, ei mihi videntur fabulam aetatis peregisse, nec tamquam inexercitati histriones in extremo actu corruisse.

reserved for visiting Spartan delegates, each of them rose and invited him to sit down.

64. This action was heartily applauded by the whole crowd, which prompted one of the Spartans to say: "These Athenians know what good behavior is, but they don't practice it."

There are many admirable customs among our own board of augurs, but one particularly relevant to our discussion is the tradition that gives the members precedence in speaking according to age. This takes priority above official rank and even above those who are serving as the highest magistrates. What sensual pleasures could be compared to the rewards such influence bestows? It seems to me that those who make good use of such rewards are like actors who have played well to the end their role in the drama

65. At sunt morosi et anxii et iracundi et difficiles senes: si quaerimus, etiam avari; sed haec morum vitia sunt, non senectutis, ac morositas tamen et ea vitia quae dixi habent aliquid excusationis, non illius quidem iustae sed quae probari posse videatur; contemni se putant, despici, illudi; praeterea in fragili corpore odiosa omnis offensio est. Quae tamen omnia dulciora fiunt et moribus bonis et artibus; idque cum in vita, tum in scena intellegi potest ex eis fratribus qui in Adelphis sunt. Quanta in altero diritas, in altero comitas! Sic se res habet; ut enim non omne vinum, sic non omnis natura vetustate coacescit. Severitatem in senectute probo, sed eam sicut alia modicam, acerbitatem nullo modo.

of life, and not like incompetent players who fall apart in the last act.

65. But some will say old people are morose, anxious, ill-tempered, and hard to please. And when we look closely, some of them are miserly as well. But these are faults of character, not of age. Besides, moroseness and the other faults I have mentioned have an arguable excuse in the aged, though perhaps not a very good one. After all, old people imagine themselves ignored, despised, and mocked. And granted, a fragile body is easily hurt. But all these troubles of age can be eased by a decent and enlightened character. We can see this in real life as well as on stage in Terence's *Adelphi* brothers.[73] One of them is most disagreeable while the other is quite pleasant. The truth is that a person's character, like wine, does not necessarily grow sour with age. Austerity

66. Avaritia vero senilis quid sibi velit non intellego: potest enim quidquam esse absurdius quam quo viae minus restet eo plus viatici quaerere?

Quarta restat causa, quae maxime angere atque sollicitam habere nostram aetatem videtur: appropinquatio mortis, quae certe a senectute non potest esse longe. O miserum senem, qui mortem contemnendam esse in tam longa aetate non viderit! Quae aut plane neglegenda est si omnino exstinguit animum, aut etiam optanda si aliquo eum deducit ubi sit futurus aeternus; atqui tertium certe nihil inveniri potest.

in old age is proper enough, but like everything else it should be in moderation. Sourness of disposition is never a virtue. As for miserliness in the old, what purpose it could serve I don't understand.

66. What could be more ridiculous than for a traveler to add to his baggage at the end of a journey?

Death Is Not to Be Feared

We must finally consider the fourth objection to growing old—an objection that seems especially calculated to cause worry and distress to a man of my years. I speak of the nearness of death. When a person is old, there is certainly no doubt that death cannot be far away.

Wretched indeed is the man who in the course of a long life has not learned that death is nothing to be feared. For death

67. Quid igitur timeam, si aut non miser post mortem aut beatus etiam futurus sum? Quamquam quis est tam stultus, quamvis sit adulescens, cui sit exploratum se ad vesperum esse victurum? Quin etiam aetas illa multo plures quam nostra casus mortis habet: facilius in morbos incidunt adulescentes, gravius aegrotant, tristius curantur. Itaque pauci veniunt ad senectutem; quod ni ita accideret, melius et prudentius viveretur; mens enim et ratio et consilium in senibus est, qui si nulli fuissent, nullae omnino civitates fuissent. Sed redeo ad mortem impendentem: quod est istud crimen senectutis,

either completely destroys the human soul, in which case it is negligible, or takes the soul to a place where it can live forever, which makes it desirable. There is no third possibility.

67. Why should I be afraid then, since after death I will be either not unhappy or happy?

Besides, who even among the young would be foolish enough to believe with absolute confidence that he will be alive when evening comes? Young people are much more likely than the old to suffer death by accident. They also fall sick more easily, suffer more intently, and are harder to cure. That is why so few young people arrive at old age. If so many didn't die young, we would have a wiser and more prudent population. For reason and good judgment are

cum id ei videatis cum adulescentia esse commune?

68. Sensi ego in optimo filio, tu in exspectatis ad amplissimam dignitatem fratribus, Scipio, mortem omni aetati esse communem. At sperat adulescens diu se victurum, quod sperare idem senex non potest. Insipienter sperat. Quid enim stultius quam incerta pro certis habere, falsa pro veris? At senex ne quod speret quidem habet. At est eo meliore condicione quam adulescens, cum id quod ille sperat hic consecutus est: ille vult diu vivere, hic diu vixit.

found in the old. If there had never been any old people, states would never have existed.

But I return now to the closeness of death. Why do you say it is a reproach to old age when you see it is also common among the young?

68. I have felt this keenly myself with the loss of my dear son, as have you, Scipio, with the death of your two brothers, young men destined for greatness. But you may argue that young people can hope to live a long time, whereas old people cannot. Such hope is not wise, for what is more foolish than to mistake something certain for what is uncertain, or something false for what is true? You might also say that an old man has nothing at all to hope for. But he in fact possesses something better than a young person. For what youth longs for, old age has attained. A young person hopes

69. Quamquam o di boni! Quid est in hominis natura diu? Da enim supremum tempus, exspectemus Tartessiorum regis aetatem (fuit enim, ut scriptum video, Arganthonius quidam Gadibus, qui octoginta regnavit annos, centum viginti vixit), sed mihi ne diuturnum quidem quidquam videtur in quo est aliquid extremum; cum enim id advenit, tum illud quod praeteriit effluxit; tantum remanet quod virtute et recte factis consecutus sis. Horae quidem cedunt et dies et menses et anni; nec praeteritum tempus umquam revertitur, nec quid sequatur sciri potest; quod cuique temporis ad vivendum datur, eo debet esse contentus.

70. Neque enim histrioni ut placeat peragenda fabula est, modo in quocumque

to have a long life, but an old man has already had one.

69. But, good gods, what in our human world ever lasts a long time? Let us assume the longest life possible, so that we may hope to reach the age of that king of Tartessus I have read about—a certain Arganthonius of Gades who reigned for eighty years and lived to the age of one hundred and twenty.[74] But to me nothing that has an end seems long. For when that end comes, all that came before is gone. All that remains then are the good and worthy deeds you have done in your life. Hours and days, months and years flow by, but the past returns no more and the future we cannot know. We should be content with whatever time we are given to live.

70. An actor does not need to remain on stage throughout a play. It is enough that

fuerit actu probetur, neque sapientibus usque ad 'plaudite' veniendum est; breve enim tempus aetatis satis longum est ad bene honesteque vivendum. Sin processerit longius, non magis dolendum est, quam agricolae dolent praeterita verni temporis suavitate aestatem autumnumque venisse. Ver enim tamquam adulescentiam significat, ostenditque fructus futuros; reliqua autem tempora demetendis fructibus et percipiendis accommodata sunt.

71. Fructus autem senectutis est, ut saepe dixi, ante partorum bonorum memoria et copia. Omnia autem quae secundum naturam fiunt sunt habenda in bonis; quid est autem tam secundum naturam quam senibus emori? Quod idem contingit adulescentibus adversante et repugnante natura. Itaque adulescentes mihi mori sic videntur

he appears in the appropriate acts. Like-wise, a wise man need not stay on the stage of this world until the audience applauds at the end. The time allotted to our lives may be short, but it is long enough to live honestly and decently. If by chance we enjoy a longer life, we have no reason to be more sorrowful than a farmer when a pleasant springtime turns to summer and autumn. Spring is like youth with the promise of fruits to come. Our later years are the seasons of harvesting and storing away.

71. The particular fruit of old age, as I have said, is the memory of the abundant blessings of what has come before.

Everything that is in accord with nature should be considered good. And what could be more proper in the natural course of life than for the old to die? When young people die, nature rebels and fights against this fate.

ut cum aquae multitudine flammae vis op-
primitur, senes autem sic ut cum sua sponte
nulla adhibita vi consumptus ignis exstinguitur; et quasi poma ex arboribus cruda si
sunt vix evelluntur, si matura et cocta deci-
dunt, sic vitam adulescentibus vis aufert,
senibus maturitas; quae quidem mihi tam
iucunda est, ut quo propius ad mortem ac-
cedam, quasi terram videre videar aliquan-
doque in portum ex longa navigatione esse
venturus.

72. Senectutis autem nullus est certus ter-
minus, recteque in ea vivitur quoad munus
offici exsequi et tueri possit et tamen mortem contemnere; ex quo fit ut animosior
etiam senectus sit quam adulescentia et for-
tior. Hoc illud est quod Pisistrato tyranno a

A young person dying reminds me of a fire extinguished by a deluge. But when an old person dies, it is like a flame that diminishes gradually and flickers away of its own accord with no force applied after its fuel has been used up. In the same way, green apples are hard to pick from a tree, but when ripe and ready they fall to the ground by themselves. So death comes to the young with force, but to the old when the time is right. To me there is great comfort in this idea, so that as death grows nearer, the more I feel like a traveler who at last sees the land of his home port after a long voyage.

72. But old age has no fixed term. A man should live on as long as he is able to fulfill his duties and obligations, holding death of no account. In this way, old age is more spirited and full of courage than youth. This explains why Solon was able to answer

Solone responsum est, cum illi quaerenti, qua tandem re fretus sibi tam audaciter obsisteret, respondisse dicitur: 'Senectute.' Sed vivendi est finis optimus cum integra mente certisque sensibus opus ipsa suum eadem quae coagmentavit natura dissolvit. Ut navem, ut aedificium idem destruit facillime qui construxit, sic hominem eadem optime quae conglutinavit natura dissolvit; iam omnis conglutinatio recens aegre, inveterata facile divellitur. Ita fit ut illud breve vitae reliquum nec avide appetendum senibus nec sine causa deserendum sit.

73. Vetatque Pythagoras iniussu imperatoris, id est dei, de praesidio et statione vitae decedere.

Pisistratus as he did when the tyrant asked what support he relied on to stubbornly oppose him as he did.[75] Solon simply said: "Old age."

The best end of life comes with a clear mind and sound body, when nature herself dissolves the work she has created. The right person to take apart a ship or a house is the man who built it. Likewise, nature best brings an end to a person she has so skillfully put together. A new building is hard to destroy, but an old house comes down easily.

Therefore, old people should not cling greedily to whatever bit of life they have left, nor should they give it up without good reason.

73. Pythagoras says we should not abandon our sentry post in this life until God, our commander, gives the order.[76] The wise

Solonis quidem sapientis est elogium
quo se negat velle suam mortem dolore amicorum et lamentis vacare; vult, credo, se
esse carum suis; sed haud scio an melius
Ennius:

Nemo me lacrumis decoret neque funera
 fletu
faxit.

74. Non censet lugendam esse mortem,
quam immortalitas consequatur. Iam sensus moriendi aliquis esse potest, isque ad
exiguum tempus, praesertim seni; post mortem quidem sensus aut optandus aut nullus
est. Sed hoc meditatum ab adulescentia debet
esse, mortem ut neglegamus; sine qua med-
itatione tranquillo esse animo nemo potest.

Solon wrote a poem in which he hopes that his friends will grieve and mourn him when he is gone. No doubt he wanted to show how much he was valued by them. But I think Ennius had a better idea when he said:

I do not wish anyone to weep for me,
nor any lamentations at my funeral.

He does not think that death should be a cause of grief since it is followed by eternal life.

74. Now, it is true that the process of dying itself may involve some unpleasant sensations, but these are fleeting, especially for the old. Then, after death, either the experience is pleasant or there is nothing at all. We should keep this in mind from our youth so that we do not fear death, since without this belief there can be no peace of

Moriendum enim certe est, et incertum an hoc ipso die; mortem igitur omnibus horis impendentem timens, qui poterit animo consistere?

75. De qua non ita longa disputatione opus esse videtur, cum recorder non Lucium Brutum qui in liberanda patria est interfectus, non duos Decios qui ad voluntariam mortem cursum equorum incitaverunt, non Marcum Atilium qui ad supplicium est profectus ut fidem hosti datam conservaret, non duos Scipiones qui iter Poenis vel corporibus suis obstruere voluerunt, non avum tuum Lucium Paulum qui morte luit conlegae in Cannensi ignominia temeritatem, non Marcum Marcellum cuius interitum ne crudelissimus quidem hostis honore sepulturae carere passus est, sed legiones nostras, quod scripsi in Originibus, in eum locum

mind. We know that we cannot escape death—in fact, it may come for us this very day. Therefore, since death threatens us at every hour, how can anyone who is afraid of it have a steadfast soul?

75. I don't need to prove this point to you with lengthy examples. It's enough to remember Lucius Brutus, who was killed bringing freedom to his country.[77] Or the two Decii, who willingly rode full speed to their deaths.[78] Or Marcus Atilius, who for the sake of keeping his pledge to the enemy returned to them to be tortured.[79] Or the two Scipios, who freely blocked the Carthaginian advance with their own bodies.[80] Or, Scipio, your own grandfather Lucius Paullus, who during the shameful defeat at Cannae gave his own life to atone for his colleague's foolishness.[81] Or Marcus Marcellus, who was given funeral honors even

saepe profectas alacri animo et erecto, unde se redituras numquam arbitrarentur. Quod igitur adulescentes, et ei quidem non solum indocti sed etiam rustici contemnunt, id docti senes extimescent?

76. Omnino ut mihi quidem videtur, studiorum omnium satietas vitae facit satietatem. Sunt pueritiae studia certa: num igitur ea desiderant adulescentes? Sunt ineuntis adulescentiae: num ea constans iam requirit aetas quae media dicitur? Sunt etiam eius aetatis: ne ea quidem quaeruntur in senectute; sunt extrema quaedam studia senectutis: ergo ut superiorum aetatum studia occidunt, sic occidunt etiam senectutis; quod cum evenit, satietas vitae tempus maturum mortis adfert.

by a pitiless enemy.[82] Or consider our legions that—as I have discussed in my own book on Roman history—have often marched with good cheer and enthusiasm into perils from which they had no hope of returning. Therefore, should wise old men fear death when it is discounted as nothing even by rustic and uneducated young soldiers?

76. It seems to me that you have had enough of life when you have had your fill of all its activities. Little boys enjoy certain things, but older youths do not yearn for these. Young adulthood has its delights, but middle age does not desire them. There are also pleasures of middle age, but these are not sought in old age. And so, just as the pleasures of earlier ages fall away, so do those of old age. When this happens, you have had enough of life and it is time for you to pass on.

77. Non enim video cur quid ipse sentiam de morte non audeam vobis dicere, quod eo cernere mihi melius videor, quo ab ea propius absum. Ego vestros patres, Publi Scipio tuque, Gai Laeli, viros clarissimos mihique amicissimos, vivere arbitror, et eam quidem vitam quae est sola vita nominanda; nam dum sumus inclusi in his compagibus corporis, munere quodam necessitatis et gravi opere perfungimur. Est enim animus caelestis, ex altissimo domicilio depressus et quasi demersus in terram, locum divinae naturae aeternitatique contrarium. Sed credo deos immortalis sparsisse animos in corpora humana, ut essent qui terras tuerentur, quique caelestium ordinem contemplantes, imitarentur eum vitae modo atque constantia. Nec me solum ratio ac disputatio impulit ut ita crederem, sed nobilitas etiam summorum philosophorum et auctoritas.

77. Let me tell you what I think about death, since the closer I draw to it the more I seem to understand it. I believe that your father, Scipio, and yours as well, Laelius—both of them illustrious men dear to me—are still alive and indeed living the only life worthy of the name. For while we are trapped within these earthly frames of ours, we carry out a heavy labor imposed on us by fate. Indeed, the soul is a heavenly thing come down from the celestial realm, pressed down and plunged into the earth, contrary to its divine and eternal nature. But I believe the immortal gods planted souls in human bodies to have beings who would care for the earth and who would contemplate the divine order and imitate it in the moderation and discipline of their own lives.

I haven't come to this belief solely by my own reasoning and logic, but with the

78. Audiebam Pythagoram Pythagore-
osque, incolas paene nostros, qui essent
Italici philosophi quondam nominati, numquam dubitasse quin ex universa mente
divina delibatos animos haberemus; demon-
strabantur mihi praeterea quae Socrates su-
premo vitae die de immortalitate aminorum
disseruisset, is qui esset omnium sapientissimus oraculo Apollinis iudicatus. Quid
multa? Sic persuasi mihi, sic sentio: cum
tanta celeritas animorum sit, tanta memoria
praeteritorum futurorumque prudentia, tot
artes, tantae scientiae, tot inventa, non posse
eam naturam quae res eas contineat esse
mortalem; cumque semper agitetur animus,
nec principium motus habeat quia se ipse
moveat, ne finem quidem habiturum esse
motus quia numquam se ipse sit relicturus;

guidance of the most noble and authoritative thinkers.

78. I used to hear that Pythagoras and his disciples—practically fellow countrymen of ours since they were known as the "Italian philosophers"—never doubted that our souls were derived from a divine, universal intelligence.[83] I also had before me the arguments about the immortality of the soul made by Socrates on the last day of his life—and the oracle of Apollo proclaimed him to be the wisest person alive.

Why should I say more? I believe and am convinced that since humans function at lightning speed, have remarkable memory of the past and knowledge of things to come, and possess amazing ability in art, science, and the capacity for discovery, the nature of their souls cannot be mortal. Moreover, since human souls are constantly

et cum simplex animi natura esset, neque
haberet in se quidquam admixtum dispar
sui atque dissimile, non posse eum dividi;
quod si non posset, non posse interire; mag-
noque esse argumento homines scire plera-
que antequam nati sint, quod iam pueri
cum artes difficiles discant, ita celeriter res
innumerabilis arripiant, ut eas non tum primum accipere videantur sed reminisci et
recordari. Haec Platonis fere.

79. Apud Xenophontem autem moriens
Cyrus maior haec dicit:

'Nolite arbitrari, O mihi carissimi filii,
me, cum a vobis discessero, nusquam aut
nullum fore. Nec enim dum eram vobiscum animum meum videbatis, sed eum esse
in hoc corpore ex eis rebus quas gerebam

in self-created motion, there can be no end to this movement nor can it ever leave itself. Also, since the soul is of a single substance and has nothing else mixed with it, it cannot be divided and therefore cannot perish. Another strong argument is that our knowledge of many things existed before we were born, as evidenced by the way that children can study and quickly master difficult subjects as if they were not learning them for the first time but recalling what they already knew. This is what Plato believes.[84]

79. In Xenophon, the dying Cyrus the Elder says the following:[85]

"My dearest sons, do not think that when I have departed from you I have ceased to exist. Even while I have been with you, you have not seen my soul, but you knew it was in my body from the deeds that I have done.

intellegebatis: eundem igitur esse creditote, etiamsi nullum videbitis.

80. Nec vero clarorum virorum post mortem honores permanerent, si nihil eorum ipsorum animi efficerent quo diutius memoriam sui teneremus. Mihi quidem numquam persuaderi potuit, animos dum in corporibus essent mortalibus vivere, cum excessissent ex eis emori, nec vero tum animum esse insipientem cum ex insipienti corpore evasisset, sed cum omni admixtione corporis liberatus, purus et integer esse coepisset, tum esse sapientem. Atque etiam cum hominis natura morte dissolvitur, ceterarum rerum perspicuum est quo quaeque discedat, abeunt enim illuc omnia unde orta sunt: animus autem solus nec cum adest nec cum discedit apparet. Iam vero videtis nihil esse morti tam simile quam somnum.

Therefore, do not stop believing even if you will see nothing.

80. "The glory of famous men would not continue after their deaths if no part of their souls survived to preserve their memories among us. I could never be persuaded that souls which dwell in human bodies perish when they leave those bodies. Nor can I believe that the soul is incapable of thought when it departs an unthinking corpse. To the contrary, when it is freed from its bonds to the body, only then can it become pure, undefiled, and truly wise. We can see that when a body dies and decays, all its elements return to their origins. The soul alone remains invisible both when the body is alive and when it has passed away.

81. Atqui dormientium animi maxime
declarant divinitatem suam; multa enim,
cum remissi et liberi sunt, futura prospici-
unt: ex quo intellegitur quales futuri sint
cum se plane corporum vinculis relaxaver-
int. Quare si haec ita sunt, sic me colitote'
inquit, 'ut deum: sin una est interiturus animus cum corpore, vos tamen deos verentes
qui hanc omnem pulchritudinem tuentur et
regunt, memoriam nostri pie inviolateque
servabitis.'

82. Cyrus quidem haec moriens; nos, si
placet, nostra videamus. Nemo umquam
mihi, Scipio, persuadebit aut patrem tuum

81. "You can see that nothing is more like death than sleep, yet it is while we are sleeping that our souls most clearly show their divine nature. When the soul is free and unfettered in sleep, it is then that it can see most clearly into the future. This gives us a hint of what our souls will be able to do when they are no longer tied to the body.

"If what I have said is true, then you can cherish me like a god after I die. But if I am wrong and my soul will perish with my body, then at least you can dutifully and inviolably honor my memory, being men who fear the gods that care for and rule over this beautiful world."

These were Cyrus's words as he lay dying. Now let me tell you what I think.

82. No one will ever convince me, Scipio, that your father Paullus, or your two grandfathers Paullus and Africanus, or the father

Paulum, aut duos avos, Paulum et Africa-
num, aut Africani patrem, aut patruum, aut
multos praestantis viros quos enumerare
non est necesse, tanta esse conatos, quae
ad posteritatis memoriam pertinerent, nisi
animo cernerent posteritatem ad se ipsos
pertinere. An censes (ut de me ipse aliquid
more senum glorier) me tantos labores di-
urnos nocturnosque domi militiaeque sus-
cepturum fuisse, si eisdem finibus gloriam
meam quibus vitam essem terminaturus?
Nonne melius multo fuisset otiosam aetatem
et quietam sine ullo labore et contentione
traducere? Sed nescio quo modo animus
erigens se posteritatem ita semper prospi-
ciebat, quasi cum excessisset e vita, tum
denique victurus esset. Quod quidem ni ita
se haberet ut animi inmortales essent, haud
optimi cuiusque animus maxime ad inmor-
talitatem et gloriam niteretur.

and uncle of Africanus, or many other famous men too numerous to name would ever have attempted such mighty deeds remembered by posterity unless they believed that the future belonged to them.

And—to say a few boastful words about myself, as old men often will—do you think that I would have labored so hard day and night, at home and in wars abroad, if I believed that the end of this earthly life would mark the limit of my fame? If that were the case, surely I would have done much better to have led a quiet and peaceful life free from labor and strife. But somehow my soul, raising itself up, always with an eye to the future, knew that true life would begin only after my death. If the soul were not immortal, why would our finest men strive so hard for glory?

83. Quid quod sapientissimus quisque aequissimo animo moritur, stultissimus iniquissimo? Nonne vobis videtur is animus qui plus cernat et longius videre se ad meliora proficisci, ille autem cui obtusior sit acies non videre? Equidem efferor studio patres vestros quos colui et dilexi videndi, neque vero eos solos convenire aveo quos ipse cognovi, sed illos etiam de quibus audivi et legi et ipse conscripsi. Quo quidem me proficiscentem haud sane quid facile retraxerit nec tamquam Peliam recoxerit; et si quis deus mihi largiatur ut ex hac aetate repuerascam et in cunis vagiam, valde recusem, nec vero velim quasi decurso spatio ad carceres a calce revocari.

83. And why is it that the wisest among us die most calmly, while the foolish die in the most distress? Isn't it that the soul of the wise man, with a keener and clearer view, sees that it is setting out for a better world, whereas the foolish soul with its duller vision cannot see where it is going?

Indeed, my dear Scipio and Laelius, I am carried away by my desire to see your fathers again, men I both respected and loved. I am also eager to see others I have known and many I have never met, men I have heard and read and written about. And once I have set out on that journey, no one will ever drag or boil me back to this life, as if I were Pelias.[86] Truly, if some god graciously granted that I could put aside my years and start over, crying in my cradle again, I would vehemently refuse. Since I

84. Quid habet enim vita commodi? Quid non potius laboris? Sed habeat sane, habet certe tamen aut satietatem aut modum. Non libet enim mihi deplorare vitam, quod multi et ei docti saepe fecerunt, neque me vixisse paenitet, quoniam ita vixi ut non frustra me natum existimem; et ex vita ita discedo tamquam ex hospitio, non tamquam domo: commorandi enim natura devorsorium nobis, non habitandi dedit. O praeclarum diem, cum ad illud divinum animorum concilium coetumque proficiscar cumque ex hac turba et conluvione discedam! Proficiscar enim non ad eos solum viros de quibus ante dixi, verum etiam ad Catonem meum, quo nemo vir melior natus est, nemo pietate praestantior; cuius a me corpus est crematum, quod contra decuit

have almost finished my race, why would I want to be called back to the starting line?

84. For what are the advantages to life—or rather, what troubles doesn't it have? Of course there are good things about life, but still there comes a time when we have had enough. No, don't count me among the large and learned population of cynics who despise life. I have no regret that I have lived, and I like to think that I was born into this world for a purpose, so that I depart from life as if from an inn, not a house. Nature gives us our bodies to abide in only for a time as guests, not to make our home.

What a wonderful day it will be when I set out to join that divine assembly of souls and leave behind this world of pain and pollution. For I shall set off to see not only those men I have mentioned before but my own son Cato—no better or more devoted

ab illo meum; animus vero, non me deser-
ens sed respectans, in ea profecto loca
discessit quo mihi ipsi cernebat esse veniendum. Quem ego meum casum fortiter ferre
visus sum, non quo aequo animo ferrem, sed
me ipse consolabar existimans non longin-
quum inter nos digressum et discessum fore.

85. His mihi rebus, Scipio, id enim te
cum Laelio admirari solere dixisti, levis est
senectus; nec solum non molesta, sed etiam
iucunda. Quod si in hoc erro, qui animos
hominum immortalis esse credam, libenter
erro, nec mihi hunc errorem quo delector,
dum vivo, extorqueri volo; sin mortuus
ut quidam minuti philosophi censent nihil
sentiam, non vereor ne hunc errorem meum
philosophi mortui irrideant. Quod si non
sumus inmortales futuri, tamen exstingui

man was ever born. Yet it was I who burned his body on the funeral pyre rather than he mine, as would have been fitting. Still, his soul is not altogether gone but always looking back, waiting for me in that place where it knows I too shall go. People think that I have borne his loss bravely. No, I have felt terrible pain, but I have consoled myself that our separation would not be forever.

85. You said at the beginning of our discussion, Scipio, that old age seems to sit lightly upon me and that this has been a cause of wonder to you and Laelius. I have told you how old age can be not only not burdensome but even enjoyable. And if I'm wrong in my belief that souls are immortal, then gladly do I err, for this belief, which I hope to maintain as long as I live, makes me happy. If, as certain small-minded philosophers believe, I shall feel nothing at all after

homini suo tempore optabile est; nam habet natura, ut aliarum omnium rerum, sic vivendi modum; senectus autem aetatis est peractio tamquam fabulae, cuius defatigationem fugere debemus praesertim adiuncta satietate.

Haec habui, de senectute quae dicerem: ad quam utinam perveniatis, ut ea quae ex me audistis re experti probare possitis.

death, then at least I don't have to worry that they will be there to mock me after they die!

If we are not immortal, nonetheless it is desirable that we should die at the proper time. For as nature has set the boundaries for everything else, so too has she set the limits of life. Old age is the final act in the play of life. When we have had enough and are weary, it is time to go.

This, my young friends, is what I believe about old age. May you both live long enough to see it and to prove by experience that the words I have spoken are true.

NOTES

Latin text by permission of Oxford University Press. © Oxford University Press. M. Tullius Ciceronis, *De Re Publica, De Legibus, Cato Maior de Senectute, Laelius de Amicitia*, edited by J.G.F. Powell. Oxford: Oxford University Press, 2006.

1. Cicero is quoting here and in the lines just below from the *Annals*, an epic history of Rome by the second-century BC Latin poet Ennius. Ennius's lines are addressed to the Roman general Flamininus, who fought against Philip V of Macedonia in 197 BC. Cicero plays on the shared first names of *Titus* Quinctius Flamininus and his own friend *Titus* Pomponius Atticus, to whom this work is dedicated.

2. Cicero's friend added the cognomen *Atticus* to his name from Attica, the region around his beloved Athens.

3. At the time this book was written, Atticus was sixty-five, Cicero sixty-two.

4. This Aristo was probably a third-century BC philosopher from the Greek island of Ceos. Tithonus was a mythical prince of Troy to whom Zeus, at the request of Eos, goddess of the dawn, gave immortality—but not eternal youth. When he grew old and senile, he shriveled away until nothing was left of him but a withered husk and his creaking voice.

5. Marcus Porcius Cato (234–149 BC) was a famously stern Roman statesman, farmer, soldier, and writer much admired by Cicero. In the year this book is set (150 BC), Cato is eighty-four, quite elderly for an ancient Roman. His young companions are Scipio Aemilianus, who would destroy Carthage in the Third Punic War four years later, and Gaius Laelius, the chief speaker in Cicero's dialogue *On Friendship*.

6. An enormous volcano in eastern Sicily.

7. A reference to either Cato's reputation as *sapiens* ("wise"), as seen elsewhere in Cicero (e.g., *On Friendship* 6), or popular etymology linking the name *Cato* with *catus* ("clever").

8. In Greek mythology, the race of giants rose up against the gods of Olympus only to be defeated.

9. Both Salinator and Albinus were consuls a few years after Cato's own consulship.

10. Themistocles was the leader of Athens during its victory over the Persian fleet at Salamis in 480 BC. Seriphos was a small, unimportant island in the Aegean Sea.

11. Quintus Fabius Maximus retook Tarentum in southern Italy in 209 BC during the Second Punic War. Know by his critics as the Delayer for his cautious but effective strategy in defeating Hannibal, he was consul five times and dictator twice before he died in 203 BC.

12. The Cincian Law (204 BC) prohibited gifts that might interfere with the administration of justice, including lawyer payments by clients.

13. A slip by Cicero. It was not actually Marcus Livius Salinator who lost Tarentum but a relative of his, Marcus Livius Macatus.

14. Flaminius proposed this law to settle Roman citizens on public lands in northern Italy.

15. Both the ancient Greeks and Romans practiced augury—divination by observing birds—to determine if the gods approved of their actions. In Rome the system was governed by a college of augurs who were chosen for life.

16. Student of Socrates and one of the most famous and influential philosophers of antiquity (c. 427–347 BC).

17. Athenian orator and teacher of rhetoric (436–338 BC).

18. Greek sophist and teacher of rhetoric from Sicily (*c.* 485–*c.* 380 BC).

19. A law passed in 169 BC restricting inheritance by women.

20. Lucius Aemilius Paullus, who defeated the Macedonians at the Battle of Pydna in 168 BC.

21. Gaius Fabricius Luscinus (consul in 282 and 278 BC) was famed for his incorruptibility. Manius Curius Dentatus, four-time consul, ended the Third Samnite War in 290 BC. Tiberius Coruncanius triumphed over the Etruscans and was consul in 280 BC.

22. Appius Claudius Caecus was consul in 307 and 296 BC. Pyrrhus, king of Epirus, helped defeat the Romans in battle in 280 BC.

23. Cato was famous for repeatedly declaring before the Senate that Carthage must be destroyed.

24. The Senate (*Senatus*) was the assembly of the leading *senes* ("old men, elders").

25. Naevius lived in the third century BC and was one of the earliest Latin playwrights.

26. Aristides, the bitter enemy of Themistocles, was the son of Lysimachus.

27. Famous Athenian playwright of the fifth century BC.

28. Simonides (sixth/fifth centuries BC), lyric poet; Stesichorus (early sixth century BC), lyric poet; Pythagoras (late sixth century BC), mathematician and philosopher; Democritus (fifth/fourth centuries BC), philosopher and formulator of the atomic theory; Xenocrates (fourth century BC), philosopher; Zeno (fifth century BC), philosopher; Cleanthes (*c.* 331–232 BC), philosopher; Diogenes of Babylon (*c.* 240–152 BC), philosopher who visited Rome in 156–155 BC.

29. Roman comic poet of the second century BC.

30. Athenian statesman and lawgiver (*c.* 638–558 BC).

31. Famous sixth-century BC wrestler and six-time victor in the Olympic Games.

32. Sextus Aelius Paetus (consul 198 BC), commentator on the ancient Twelve Tables of Roman law; Publius Licinius Crassus Dives (consul 205 BC).

33. Gnaeus Cornelius Scipio Calvus and his younger brother Publius Cornelius Scipio were both Roman generals who died (211 BC) fighting the Carthaginians in Spain. Lucius Aemilius Paullus, Roman consul and general, died in 216 BC at the Battle of Cannae. Publius Cornelius Scipio Africanus defeated Hannibal in the Battle of Zama (202 BC) to end the Second Punic War.

34. Cyrus the Great (sixth century BC) was founder of the Persian Empire. Xenophon (*Cyropaedia* 8.7) says that he died of old

age, but other accounts indicate he died in battle against the Scythians.

35. Lucius Caecilius Metellus, consul in 251 and 247 BC.

36. According to Homer, the elderly Nestor ruled the kingdom of Pylos and was a key advisor to Agamemnon, leader of the Greek forces who waged war on Troy.

37. *Iliad* 1.249.

38. After Achilles, Ajax was the most formidable of the Greek warriors.

39. Cato was sent to Greece in 191 BC with the consul Manius Acilius Glabrio to oppose an invasion by Antiochus III, ruler of the Seleucid Empire. In that same year, they defeated Antiochus at the pass of Thermopylae, where the Spartans had faced the Persian invaders three centuries earlier.

40. An otherwise unknown soldier of Cato's time famed for his strength.

41. King of the Numidians (died 148 BC) and ally of the Romans in the Second Punic War against Carthage.

42. The Scipio of this dialogue was adopted by Publius Cornelius Scipio, the son of celebrated Publius Cornelius Scipio Africanus.

43. A now-lost history of Rome from its beginnings until the second century BC.

44. Archytas, who was active in the first half of the fourth century BC, was a Pythagorean philosopher, mathematician, astronomer, and friend of Plato.

45. A shameful defeat of the Romans in 321 BC.

46. This is doubtful, since Plato would have been almost eighty years old at this date (349 BC).

47. Cato did this when he was censor in 184 BC, along with Lucius Valerius Flaccus.

48. Cineas, a student of the Athenian orator Demosthenes, was employed by Pyrrhus to negotiate with the Romans.

49. The philosopher Epicurus (341–270 BC).
50. Publius Decius Mus died leading the Romans at the Battle of Sentinum (295 BC).
51. Plato *Timaeus* 69d.
52. Duilius beat the Carthaginians off Mylae in Sicily during the First Punic War (260 BC).
53. The eastern goddess Cybele, whose cult based near Mount Ida in Asia Minor came to Rome when Cato was quaestor (204 BC).
54. Cicero is here translating the Greek words *synposion* (hence the English "symposium") and *syndeipnon*.
55. Xenophon *Symposium* 2.26.
56. Plato *Republic* 329b.
57. Actor and producer of the comedies of Terence in the second century BC.
58. Plautus (early second century BC) was one of the first and most successful Roman writers of comedies.

59. Livius Andronicus (*c.* 280–200 BC) was a freed Greek slave who translated Homer's *Odyssey* into Latin and became an influential Roman playwright.

60. Gaius Claudius Cento and Marcus Sempronius Tuditanus were consuls in 240 BC.

61. Publius Cornelius Scipio Nasica Corculum, consul in 162 and 155 BC, and cousin by adoption of the Scipio in this dialogue.

62. Cethegus was consul in 204 BC.

63. *Occatio* ("to harrow, turn the soil") actually comes from *occa* ("a hoe").

64. Cato's book *On Agriculture* survives and is a fascinating look into not only ancient farming but also early Roman society.

65. In his *Works and Days*.

66. Most modern scholars would argue that the Greek poets Homer and Hesiod were near-contemporaries (*c.* 700 BC). As for Laertes, Homer says (*Odyssey* 24.227) only that he

was digging around a plant in his vineyard, not that he was using manure.

67. Lucius Quinctius Cincinnatus was said to have been given temporary emergency powers as dictator in 458 BC to defeat the Aequi and again in 439 BC to stop Spurius from illegally seizing power in Rome. The master of the horse was a Roman dictator's second-in-command.

68. *Oeconomicus* 4.20–25. Like Plato, Xenophon was a student of Socrates and used him as a narrator in several of his works.

69. Cyrus the Younger was the son of King Darius II. He was killed in 401 BC in a battle with his brother for his father's throne—a battle in which Xenophon fought as a mercenary. Lysander (died 395 BC) was a Spartan general who had worked with the Persians to defeat Athens in the Peloponnesian War. Sardis was a Persian capital in Lydia in western Asia Minor.

70. Marcus Valerius Corvinus was reputedly Roman consul six times in the late fourth and early third centuries BC.

71. Caiatinus, consul in 258 and 254 BC, was a hero of the First Punic War.

72. Marcus Aemilius Lepidus, consul in 187 and 175 BC.

73. Theatrical work by the second-century BC Roman playwright.

74. Gades (modern Cádiz) was in the kingdom of Tartessus in southwestern Spain. The story is found in Herodotus 1.163.

75. Pisistratus was tyrant of Athens in the mid-sixth century BC.

76. Cicero here uses the Latin singular *deus* ("God" or "god") as the supreme being.

77. Lucius Junius Brutus, who became one of Rome's first consuls in 509 BC after overthrowing the last Etruscan king of Rome. He was killed while fighting an Etruscan army that was attempting to restore the kingship.

78. Father and son, both named Publius Decius Mus. The father was consul in 340 BC and deliberately sacrificed his life fighting Rome's enemies, as did his son in 295 BC.

79. Marcus Atilius Regulus (consul in 267 and 256 BC), who reportedly was captured by the Carthaginians but went to Rome to negotiate after promising his captors he would return to them to be tortured to death.

80. Publius Cornelius Scipio and Gnaeus Cornelius Scipio Calvus.

81. Lucius Aemilius Paullus died along with perhaps fifty thousand Roman soldiers at the Battle of Cannae in 216 BC after being trapped by Hannibal.

82. Marcus Claudius Marcellus, celebrated general and five-time consul, was killed in battle (208 BC) against Hannibal, who it was later said gave him funeral honors and sent his ashes back to his son.

83. Pythagoras emigrated from Samos in Greece to Croton in southern Italy.
84. *Phaedo* 72–73.
85. *Cyropaedia* 8.7.
86. In Greek mythology, Medea claimed she could restore Pelias to life by cutting him up and boiling him in a cauldron.

FURTHER READING

Cicero, Marcus Tullius. *Cato Maior de Senectute*. Edited with introduction and commentary by J.G.F. Powell. Cambridge: Cambridge University Press, 2004.

———. *How to Run a Country: An Ancient Guide for Modern Leaders*. Selected, translated, and with an introduction by Philip Freeman. Princeton: Princeton University Press, 2013.

———. *Selected Works*. Translated and introduced by Michael Grant. New York: Penguin Books, 1971.

Cicero, Quintus Tullius. *How to Win an Election: An Ancient Guide for Modern Politicians*. Translated and with an introduction by Philip Freeman. Princeton: Princeton University Press, 2012.

Everitt, Anthony. *Cicero: The Life and Times of Rome's Greatest Politician*. New York: Random House, 2001.

Gruen, Erich. *The Last Generation of the Roman Republic*. Berkeley: University of California Press, 1995.

Parkin, Tim G. *Old Age in the Roman World: A Cultural and Social History*. Baltimore: Johns Hopkins University Press, 2004.

Rawson, Elizabeth. *Cicero: A Portrait*. London: Bristol Classical Press, 1983.

Richard, Carl J. *The Founders and the Classics: Greece, Rome, and the American Enlightenment*. Cambridge, Massachusetts: Harvard University Press, 1994.

Scullard, H. H. *From the Gracchi to Nero: A History of Rome from 133 BC to AD 68*. New York: Routledge, 1982.

Syme, Ronald. *The Roman Revolution*. Oxford: Oxford University Press, 2002.